Myra Schneider is a well-known poet who has given poetry readings all over Britain and been featured on Radio 2 and Radio 4. Her seventh collection of poetry is due in 1998, and her work has been published in literary journals and national newspapers. She is a successful writing tutor who has run many writing workshops and courses. She also teaches communication and literacy to severely disabled adults.

John Killick is an author who has worked as a writer in residence in a variety of institutions. He is an international lecturer on the subject of Writing and Dementia, and he works part-time in the Dementia Services Development Centre at Stirling University. He is a past Chair and Secretary for the National Association for Writing in Education, and has run writing courses for various bodies, including the Arvon Foundation, and also promotes writing courses at the Nant Centre in North Wales.

BY MYRA SCHNEIDER

Poetry:

Fistful of Yellow Hope, Littlewood Press, 1984
Cat Therapy, Littlewood Press, 1986
Cathedral of Birds, Littlewood/Giant Steps, 1988
Opening the Ice (with Ann Dancy), Smith/Doorstep, 1990
Crossing Point, Littlewood Are, 1991
Exits, Enitharmon, 1994
The Panic Bird, Enitharmon, 1998

Fiction:

For children:
Marigold's Monster, Heinemann, 1977

For teenagers:
If Only I Could Walk, Heinemann, 1978
Will the Real Pete Roberts Stand Up?, Heinemann, 1979

BY JOHN KILLICK

Poetry:

Windhorse, Rockingham, 1996
You Are Words: Dementia Poems, Hawker, 1997

Non-fiction:

Please Give Me Back My Personality, Stirling University, 1994

Books edited:

The Times of Our Lives, Westminster Health Care, 1994
Between the Lines, Between the Bars, Other Voices, 1994
Coming of Age, Other Voices, 1997

WRITING FOR SELF-DISCOVERY

A Personal Approach to Creative Writing

MYRA SCHNEIDER
JOHN KILLICK

ELEMENT

Shaftesbury, Dorset • Rockport, Massachusetts
Melbourne, Victoria

First published in Great Britain in 1998 by
Element Books Limited
Shaftesbury, Dorset SP7 8BP

Published in the USA in 1998 by
Element Books, Inc.
PO Box 830, Rockport, MA 01966

Published in Australia in 1998 by
Element Books and distributed
by Penguin Books Australia Ltd
487 Maroondah Highway, Ringwood,
Victoria 3134

Cover design by Mark Slader
Page design by Roger Lightfoot
Phototypeset by Intype London Ltd
Printed and bound in Great Britain by J. W. Arrowsmith, Bristol

British Library Cataloguing in Publication
data available

Library of Congress Cataloging in Publication
data available

ISBN 1 86204 205 5

Contents

Acknowledgements

We particularly wish to thank Erwin Schneider for all the work he did in collating our two manuscripts.

We would also like to thank art therapist, Scilla Ansell, whose ideas contributed to 'Drawing as a Stimulus' and William Ayot who gave us helpful information.

Many thanks to everyone else who has contributed to this book.

Copyright Acknowledgements

The authors and publishers would like to thank all copyright holders, and acknowledge the following for permission to use copyright material:

Frances Angela for 'Strip Wash'

Donald Atkinson and Peterloo Poets for an extract from *A Sleep of Drowned Fathers*. Copyright © 1989 Donald Atkinson. Reproduced by permission of Peterloo Poets

William Ayot for 'Never' and 'Tears on the Drum'

Jill Bamber for 'Brailling the Sheet'

Frances Bellerby and David Higham Associates for 'A Clear Shell' from *Selected Poems*, Enitharmon Press 1986

Alison Chisholm for 'Contact' in *Staple* 38, 1997

Jonathan Davidson and Arc Publications for 'Now We are Married' and an extract from 'The Living Room' from *The Living Room*, Arc Publications 1994

Jane Duran and Enitharmon Press for 'Forty Eight' from *Breathe Now, Breathe*, Enitharmon Press 1995

Elke Dutton for 'Among Strangers'

Phoebe Hesketh and Enitharmon Press for 'Credo' and 'Widowhood' from *The Leave Train: New and Selected Poems*, Enitharmon Press 1994

Molly Holden and Carcanet Press for 'Upstairs Light' from *Selected Poems*, Carcanet Press Limited 1987

Liz Houghton for 'Caustic Soda' from *The Long Pale Corridor*, edited by Judi Benson and Agneta Falk, Bloodaxe 1996

Sue Hubbard and Enitharmon Press for 'Inheritance' from *Everything Begins with the Skin*, Enitharmon Press 1994

Jan Jenkins for 'Keeping in Touch'

Brian Jones and Carcanet Press for 'Children of Separation' from *Children of Separation*, Carcanet Press Limited 1995

Mimi Khalvati and Carcanet Press for 'Reaching the Midway Mark' from *Mirrorwork*, Carcanet Press Limited 1995

Philip Levine and Alfred A. Knopf, Inc for an extract from 'Fear and Fame' in *What Work Is*. Copyright © 1991 by Philip Levine. Reprinted by permission of Alfred A Knopf Inc

Harold Monro for 'Living' from *Collected Poems of Harold Monro*, Duckworth 1970. Reprinted by permission of Gerald Duckworth & Co Ltd

Hubert Moore and Enitharmon Press for 'Alders' from *Left-Handers*, Enitharmon Press 1995

Edwin Morgan and Carcanet Press for an extract from 'A View of Things' from *Collected Poems*, Carcanet Press, 1990

Les Murray, Carcanet Press and Farrar, Straus & Giroux, Inc. for 'Burning Want' from *Subhuman Redneck Poems*, Carcanet Press Limited 1996 and copyright © 1997 by Les Murray. Reprinted by permission of Les Murray and by permission of Farrar, Straus & Giroux, Inc

Dorothy Nimmo for 'Dream Play' from *Homewards*, Giant Steps 1987

Pascale Petit and Smith/Doorstop Books for an extract from 'Icefall Climbing in Tibet' from *Icefall Climbing*, Smith/Doorstop Books 1994

Caroline Price, Arc Publications and Rockingham Press for 'Eve of Removal' from *Thinking of the Bulldancers*, Littlewood Press 1987, and 'Pictures Against Skin' from *Pictures Against Skin*, Rockingham Press 1994

Irene Rawnsley and Arc Publications for 'Odi et Amo' from *Shall We Gather at the River*, Littlewood 1990

Mrs Ethel E Ross for the extract from *The Story and the Fable* by Edwin Muir, Hogarth Press, 1940

Colin Rowbotham and Arc Publications for 'Flowers and Thorns' and an extract from 'Missing Locks' from *Total Recall*, Littlewood Press 1987
the late Keith Spencer for 'Not By This Fire'
Isobel Thrilling and Arc Publications for an extract from 'Mother' from *Spectrum Shift*, Littlewood Press 1991
Tony Turner for 'Struggling'
Arthur Waley and HarperCollins Publishers Ltd for 'Lazy Man's Song' from *Chinese Poems*, HarperCollins Publishers, 1946
John Ward and Arc Publications for an excerpt from 'Shoes' from *The Wrong Side of Glory*, Littlewood Press 1986
Susan Wicks, Faber & Faber Limited and HarperCollins Publishers, Inc for two excerpts from 'Driving My Father' by Susan Wicks, Faber & Faber Limited, 1995. Copyright © 1996 by Susan Wicks. Reprinted by permission of BasicBooks, a division of HarperCollins Publishers, Inc
Alfred Williams and Ray Brown for extracts from *To Live It is To Know It*, Yorkshire Art Circus 1987
Frances Wilson and Rockingham Press for 'Bathing My Mother' from *Close to Home*, Rockingham Press 1993
Joy Winterbottom for 'Who's That?'

Every effort has been made to trace all copyright owners but if any have been inadvertently overlooked the authors and publishers will be pleased to make the necessary acknowledgement at the first opportunity.

Introduction

The approach to writing taken in this book is creative rather than analytical. It asks you to draw upon feelings, memories and the imagination to help you reflect upon your life-experiences. It is less concerned with explanation and assessment as a means of understanding.

This book is for anyone who wishes to use writing as a tool for self-exploration. You do not need to be an experienced writer to gain full benefit from tackling this material. However, we believe that the book will be helpful to writers who wish to deepen their work by adopting a more personal approach.

We begin with some straightforward exercises to help you to feel comfortable when writing about your feelings if this is new to you. These are followed by eight sets of techniques which we have found invaluable for exploring the self, and which we encourage you to use in the later parts of the book. The third part of the book brings into focus the influences of the individual physique and psyche and all the factors which come to bear upon us from outside. We then demonstrate how the raw material from the exercises may be extended and/or shaped into finished pieces of writing. Other possibilities for longer projects are keeping a journal and writing an autobiography and we examine these next. Lastly we take five major themes and show how various writers have treated them.

Writing for Self-Discovery is designed for individuals to use by themselves. The book has a logical structure so that it would be possible for you to work straight through it. However, because each section contains so much material, you could pick and choose exercises as you proceed. It would also be appropriate to focus upon topics which particularly interest you. As this is a source book it is worth returning after an interval and attempting new exercises. You may also find it stimulating to re-do exercises in search of new insights. We see the Flow-Writing and Clustering techniques as fundamental, and suggest that you give time to these before you go very far into the rest of the material.

We have indicated that the book is one that you can break off from and return to, but if it is possible for you to set aside regular times you will develop a writing habit, and find the process a more satisfying one. We recommend that you keep all your pieces of work together in order to preserve them, and also in case you want to develop them or use them as a future resource.

This book is not intended as therapy but it has a therapeutic element, as indeed does much writing. You will be confronting your feelings directly. Of course, each piece you write will be private unless you choose to show it to someone else. You are setting out on a valuable and exciting adventure but one which may at times be difficult and scary. Ideas may be uncovered which are hard to face. Events in your life (some half or wholly forgotten) may rise to the surface. You will have to be open with yourself. But you should be aware that if something which you feel unable to cope with presents itself you may need to seek professional help.

Although we have designed the book for individual use we are aware that groups may choose to use it, either to work through some of the main sections, or to concentrate upon specific techniques or themes. The leader of such a group will need to exercise sensitivity over confidentiality and be aware that difficult issues may arise for individuals in the group.

The pieces of writing we have used as illustrations of many of the exercises are an essential element in the book. These have largely been supplied by members of our writing groups and workshops. We should like to thank them for their contributions. Here are some comments about personal writing made by Elke Dutton:

> When I write about my life I lay claim to it and give it value. My life is then not just something that has happened to me but belongs to me. Writing helps me to stand in my own shoes. Creating finished pieces of work out of my personal world is also important, as if by giving the writing shape I also create an inner sense of completion and order.

We believe that personal writing has been much undervalued both as a potent form of self-expression and as a contribution to art.

PART ONE

Getting in Touch with Feelings

The purpose of this opening section is to encourage you to try out some different ways of writing about your feelings, thoughts and attitudes. As with the exercises that follow in later chapters the purpose is not to produce polished pieces of work but to help you to explore yourself. It doesn't matter if what you write is uneven, in notes, over the top, contradictory, not fully explained, over-explained, means nothing to anyone but you. It will be material that you can develop or refer to later on. Try out these exercises in a spirit of adventure. We hope they will whet your appetite! We suggest you work through them fairly quickly before starting on the Techniques Sections in Part Two.

EXERCISE 1: AT THIS MOMENT

This is a simple but effective way to begin writing and focusing on oneself. Sit down with your notebook and pen in a room at home or anywhere that you will feel comfortable writing. Begin by looking at your immediate surroundings. See what catches your attention. It may be the pattern on the carpet, a fly on the window pane, a dirty cup, the painting on the wall, an open door and what lies beyond it, the view outside, the overflowing wastepaper basket, a letter you forgot to post, etc. Describe two or three objects, picking out some precise details such as shape, size, colour, texture, smell. Then write briefly about one or two of these: the sounds you can hear, the warmth or coldness, the amount of light and the kind of light. Move on to describe yourself, how you are sitting, your mood, feelings, preoccupations, the thoughts that come into your head while you are doing the exercise. Write for ten minutes. Soon after she started attending a writing group Karen Taggart did this exercise. Here is an extract from it:

> The third thing is my telephone. My communication. Today I am constantly anxious for it to ring as my daughter has just arrived home from hospital after the unexpectedly difficult birth of her first child, my first grandchild. I am having to learn to become an onlooker now that she has a partner. This is a new and difficult role for me but I must learn to step back and watch. This little white machine is sitting silently and the temptation is to lift and dial. Instead I must sit and wait but I frequently glare at it, willing it to ring.

And here are the sentences with which Dave Alton began this exercise:

> There's the usual mess in the room: dead toast on a plate, a black banana skin drooped over it, socks and two beer cans on the floor, half a shelf of books on a good-natured sofa, a bleary smell. I ought to get up, open up, get out for a run but I don't feel like doing anything except warming my feet on the radiator – can't think of anything except her – why hasn't she phoned?

EXERCISE 2: PERSONAL LANDSCAPES

This is an enjoyable and often a potent way of making contact with one's past. Picture an outdoor place or landscape that was special to you in your childhood or some years back. It may be a location you saw frequently, somewhere you went occasionally, or a place you visited only once. It could be a garden, a road, a river, beach, playground, zoo, mountain, view from a window, the outside of a building, etc. Describe the place, picking out features that were important to you. Include any sounds, colours, textures and smells you remember. Explain how you felt about the place and also how you feel as you think and write about it now. Mention any incident you remember connected with the place or any other thoughts you have about it. Spend ten minutes on this exercise, more if you want to. Here is part of a personal landscape piece by Ann Farry:

> The hill at the back of the houses opposite loomed so large. As a child it became a playground, something to be conquered, afraid of, beaten. There's a small channel scored in one side just wide enough to take a sledge in winter. It's a short cut when in a rush but too black at night when its mass somehow doubles. Bracken rules the dark side, its sunny aspect worn out by us kids sliding down on tea trays – a car door once – from where nobody questioned. There are concrete steps set in further down, great grey unlooked-after teeth which scarred the undulations with harsh geometry, an area I avoid for fear of falling into the hands of the enemy – many battles over territory there.

It's interesting to note that after the second sentence Ann moved into the present tense – as if she was re-living her past.

EXERCISE 3: DESERT ISLANDS

You are marooned on a benign desert island. It is warm, without any dangerous creatures, offers plenty of easily obtainable bananas, coconuts, other fruits and fish to eat, also fresh water and tree shelter. You have time on your hands. Write for three or four minutes about each of the following:

a) What and who you would most miss, explaining why.
b) What you would be glad to get away from.

c) Which two objects you would choose to have with you from your home to make your life more bearable and give it some interest. (The phone, radio and television are not on offer!)

d) How you would cope with isolation and structure your time.

Karen Taggart also tried this exercise. Here are two extracts from it:

> Who or what would I miss most? This has to be the companionship of another human being. Therefore I would choose my daughter, my best and closest friend. If I had been asked this question five years ago my answer would have been my husband, but we are apart now and during this time my daughter and I have become much closer and I know that I would feel deeply unhappy without the warmth of her love and support [. . .]
>
> How would I cope with isolation? Badly I'm afraid, and afraid is exactly what I would be. As a way of combating this I would make friends with every living creature I could find and of course the way to do this is by feeding them. Some would talk to me and some would sing. In fact we could sing together and I could then learn to conduct my own choir with daily rehearsals!

EXERCISE 4: POSITIVE AND NEGATIVE

List three experiences you have had recently that were interesting, satisfying, illuminating or uplifting. Possibilities might be: a conversation that brought you close to someone, a discussion that brought up all sorts of ideas, a book that excited you, listening to music, helping someone, the evening sky, finishing a piece of work, an extremely funny incident, etc. Choose one of the experiences and write about it for seven minutes, concentrating on your feelings and thoughts.

Now list three recent experiences that upset, angered or disturbed you in some way. Possibilities might be: a row with someone, a problem at work, a disappointment, an illness, a loss, being misunderstood, etc. Choose one of the experiences and repeat the writing exercise.

Example

I was dizzy by the time I found the room where they did blood tests. Outside it was a waiting area full of people. I couldn't sit down, paced up and down. Frightened of a little jab, I sneered at myself. 'You're not a child of ten. You're supposed to be man of 32.'

'Something wrong?' The nurse was a slight little thing with kind eyes. I couldn't help myself: 'It's the blood, I can't bear the sight of it.'

'No problem,' she smiled. 'We'll make sure you don't see any. You'd be surprised how many we get in here like that, my little love.'

Little love! I'm over six feet. She barely reached my elbow. We both laughed and suddenly I was half crying, swaying. She sat me down with a paper cup of tea. I've never felt such a fool in my life!

Jim Johnston

EXERCISE 5: PATTERNING

Patterning is making a list in which you repeat the same form of words to introduce each item. The repetition helps release ideas and feelings and it is a chance to play with words. It is also satisfying to produce this kind of rhythmic writing which can have a very strong effect, may even be a poem! Write quickly without thinking too much and enjoy experimenting. Take one of these opening phrases and write a line with it, then add lines for six minutes: 'I want', 'I don't want', 'My life is', 'I wish I could', 'In my perfect world', 'Today I am', 'Today I am not', 'I'm going to go out there and', and 'When I reach the top of the mountain'. Here are two extracts:

> Today I am not going to climb a tower of anger.
> Today I am not going to nag the kids.

Today I am not going to be a big soft punch bag.
Today I am not going to be a humpy camel.
Today I am not going to do any cooking.

Rosemary Colehurst

I want my life back.
I want to smash your fucking face in.
I want a new job.
I want you to read me Winnie the Pooh.
I want to eat again.
I want to talk about something else.
I want you to be at the train station after work.
I want to have those children we talked about.
I want to rip the tongue out of your head.
I want you to tell me I'm beautiful, like you used to.

Maya Prausnitz

Now repeat the exercise using a feeling in the form: 'Hope is', 'Fear is', 'Anger is', 'Love is', 'Disappointment is', etc. Here is an extract from Tim Lytton's list:

Disappointment is an empty pocket.
Disappointment is voice saying: 'You're not up to it.'
Disappointment is a letter saying no.
Disappointment is a door shutting.
Disappointment is the sun dropping into the sea.

EXERCISE 6: INFLUENCES

Our attitudes and our reactions to day-to-day events are strongly influenced by our early lives. As a preliminary we'd like you to write for ten minutes without planning, what suggests itself about one of the following: a very early memory, a significant memory, your mother, father, a brother, sister, grandparent or other relative.

Example

Her hair was yellowing, lay stringy across the pillow. The room was dim, lit by a weak pool from the bedside lamp. Grandma was so thin, the cords of her neck stood out like tree roots. I was frightened by the dark hollows under her eyes and sat in a chair by the fireplace.

She turned her head. 'Come here,' she croaked and patted the bed weakly [. . .] The room was quiet except for the tick-tock of the big wooden clock on the mantelpiece. It paused, gears whirred and the quarter hour chimed. Then silence clogged the senses and choked Grandma's every breath.

'I'm dying,' and her eyes apologized. Her voice was so small and cracked that it was not Grandma at all. The room smelt of camphor and drawn browning shades, dust and stale sheets.

Ann Griswold

Outside factors and circumstances also have a profound effect on us. Choose one of these which is meaningful to you and repeat the exercise: poverty, wealth, gender, disability, town, rural area, unemployment, education, class, religion, mother tongue, prejudice. As an example here are some comments made by Alfred Williams at the beginning of his autobiography, *To Live It Is To Know It*, which he dictated to a friend:

When I were young, in the West Indies, it were a bit different from here, but the heel that we people of Jamaica was under, English people was under it just the same. But I come to know this; every country have its rich and poor, its first class, second class and third class. But the poverty stricken here, in England now, they like the middle-class to the poverty stricken in Jamaica when I were a young boy.

That heel was on the neck as far back as I remember. Say I start about 1925, when I was a little boy.

Part Two

Techniques

Flow-Writing

This technique starts from the premise that our conscious minds contain only a fraction of what is valuable about us as human beings, and that if we are to explore further we must tap that huge reservoir of ideas, images and feelings which make up our unconscious minds. To do so it is not necessary to be aware of the theories and practices of Freud and Jung (interesting though these are). It is only necessary for us to set up the procedures whereby we may regularly avail ourselves of this great resource of experience and memory. In doing so our main concern must be to dissuade the logical, analytical self from interfering. It is quite clear to us as writers that the greatest enemy of the imagination and fluency is the intellect with its incessant tinkering and evaluation of perceptions. For the purpose of this exercise we must put it aside.

By allowing ourselves to associate freely – that is to put down the first words that come into our heads, then to write down whatever these make us think of and to keep following the train of thought wherever it takes us – our deepest ideas and feelings begin to surface. When you try out this technique you may feel a strong urge to direct your writing, but resist it. Don't plan, just write down whatever comes into your head. Don't worry if you panic or dry up.

Repeat the last few words you've written until something new suggests itself, then continue.

Try not to censure anything because this interferes with the flow, holds down your inner thoughts and feelings. It doesn't matter if things come up that seem trivial or silly. Just relax. The mind operates on several planes at once; the superficial, the apparently insignificant, will lead you elsewhere if you allow it, and may even turn out to be a part of something interesting or important.

If personal, private, uncertain or difficult feelings or ideas begin to suggest themselves, feel free to write them down. This writing is for you alone – certainly at this stage. Afterwards you can decide if you want to cross it out, keep it for reference, or to explore it further and maybe develop it into a piece of prose or poetry.

Don't worry about whether you have found the exact word, whether what you are writing is logical or makes grammatical sense, is well expressed or clumsily put. Allow yourself 'to go with the flow', to enjoy splashing into words. Practise this technique. You will be surprised, excited even, by the lively unexpected powerful phrases that crop up, by the thoughts and feelings that begin to surface.

EXERCISE 7

There are various ways of starting off. One is to use a sentence opening which suggests discovery, movement, encounter or memory. Begin writing with one of these: 'I opened the door and . . .', 'For the first time in my life . . .', 'I looked down and . . .', 'I began to . . .', 'It's years since . . .', 'At first I thought . . .', 'What I wanted was . . .'. Then continue writing for five minutes.

Here are some other openings. Try two or three of them and write for between five and ten minutes. 'Coming towards me was . . .', 'What I wanted to tell you was . . .', 'The music made me feel . . .', 'I was aware of pain . . .', 'I couldn't speak because . . .', 'What I want to do is . . .', 'A long way back . . .', 'I couldn't make out . . .', 'If I'm really honest . . .', 'He/she has changed since . . .', 'When I touched . . .', 'I looked in the mirror and . . .', 'If I dared I'd . . .', 'What excites me is . . .', 'I buried it . . .'

After you've written each piece read it and underline the sentences, phrases and words that strike you because they contain a thought or feeling or a word that catches your attention, interests you or excites you. Here are extracts from three different attempts:

For the first time in my life I'm trying this and I feel foolish – not sure I can do it. I've always liked words – reading what other people have written, reading to the children – but this is supposed to be my words and thoughts. I feel afraid, at sea, yes it's like that feeling, that child's feeling when you go swimming in the sea – scared and excited at the same time, especially as the water comes up and up and you suddenly take off into swimming and it's wonderful to be in it – the colour of the clear greenish-blue water, the sun riding the surface, shells on the sand that's been ridged by the tide. Oh I want to keep floating if I can!

Susan Frost

It's years since I watched a cricket match, decades since I touched a bat. Clack of ball on willow, lying in the long grass waiting your turn, knowing, fearing it will come. 'Come on, get those pads on, you lily-livered little runt, you're not here to laze or pick daisies, you're here to make runs!' How was I to do that? I would swing the bat wildly, great scythings through the air. 'Only Connect' – surely Forster wasn't thinking of cricket? The only thing that connected was my middle stump. Help, I've made an ass of myself again! And that long walk to the pavilion, in the silence, passing through an aisle of disgruntled faces. Then the scoff: 'You'll never be a man till you can face up to a fast bowler.' Sheer nonsense – how English to take our values from competitive games! Ugh, let them all win, I say, play the game to lose, that'll show them!

Bill Lucas

I buried it in the garden, shoving the spade into the overdry earth, made a hole and when it was deep enough I buried it. What was this shapeless, inexplicable thing I was covering with clods of earth? Not a snake which is a smooth coiling thing even if it squirms, not a rag doll. When I'd covered it completely I was conscious that it was still there. Burying it was not going to get rid of it. It was at this point that I realized that the thing – the lump of it – was my feelings about her.

Celia Abbot

EXERCISE 8

Here is another way to start Flow-Writing. Write down two or three of the following: a feeling, a colour, a food, a sound, a smell, a texture, something you've said or thought today, an object you've handled, a plant you've seen, an animal, the name of a person you know or have known. Now make up a sentence using at least two of the words you've written down. Let this be the first sentence of your Flow-Writing. Any of your preliminary words may have an influence on it.

Example

Red, anger, hoot. It must be lack of confidence not anger that made him hoot. Yes, he has to be in control or he can't cope. I know that feeling exactly, that sense that I must keep hold of all ends. Red ends fraying, ends jumping out of my hands, pulling off my jacket, leaving me so exposed I will never recover. Re- cover what old cushion? Cats' hairs all over the cushion . . . and at this point the cat walks over my wallet, over the computer keys and creates a word on the screen. Words, words words. Hamlet – anger. How can I write about *my* anger?

Leigh Thomas

Again underline any sentences, phrases or words that interest you. You may want to use or refer to them later.

EXERCISE 9

If you have an idea, feeling or something on your mind you want to explore, try putting down the first sentence about it that comes into your head and then see where Flow-Writing takes you. You'll probably have your own ideas but here are some suggestions: hope, flying, swimming, difficulty, choice, panic, resentment, excitement, illness, travel, drugs, energy, disappointment, fear, climbing mountains, sharing, survival, deceit.

EXERCISE 10

Fantasy, or what Myra calls 'Alice-in-Wonderland' Flow-Writing, is fun. By opening with a nonsensical sentence we invite you to take off into the world of make-believe and enjoy finding strange word combinations or letting strange connections take control. One value of this is that the light-hearted approach encourages people to loosen up. Some of the ridiculous words and sentences allowed in are likely to be very alive. And if you 'go with the flow' central subject-matter is likely to surface. Here are some possible starters: 'Today I am a pink bicycle . . .', 'Looking up, I saw the air was out of control . . .', 'Making a nest for myself in the fur lining of the giant slipper, I . . .', ' "I'd fight back," I told the judge and hit him with the honey-pot . . .', 'The machine opened its heart and I . . .', 'You're nothing but papier maché . . .', 'I whispered to my lover . . .', 'I jumped across the gold and blue into . . .' Here is some fantasy Flow-Writing done by Myra in a few minutes.

> I discovered I was a pink bicycle riding down the silver road and my bell rang loudly at the daffodils that trumpeted at me from the roundabout. 'I am flamingo pink,' I screamed at the lamp post and it turned into an ostrich. 'Go and bury your head in the sand,' I ordered. It winked at me and suddenly stars were twinkling and darkness ran down the sky and down the steps to

my childhood seafront where the Alsatian dog lived. 'Today I
am a pink bicycle,' I whispered into his ears as he barked with
joy and he believed me and I believed myself. And now I reached
the esplanade and slithered down the crumbling steps and over
the low rock shelves that snarled words that couldn't break my
bones, and out onto the sea. My moorings were undone. I was
neither child nor adult and my saddle – my saddle glittered more
than any diamond.

EXERCISE 11

Now it's time to take the plunge and try starting without a
handle. Hopefully your unconscious mind will purr into
action. Write down the first sentence you can think of, then
continue writing for eight minutes or more if you want to.
If your mind goes completely blank try first of all writing a
sentence about something you can see and using that as
a starting point. Then try again without a prompt.

Example

Wanting a mother myself and being a mother. Care, cup balsam,
it's all right, I'm here. Crushed balsam infusion in a warm cup
and it will heal him. Then I might stroke his right hand, get on
his right side where he can still feel. Where has his left side gone?
There, on the other half of the chair, on the far side of the bed.
The dumb foot in the leaden slipper, the comb dragged through
the hair over a parting that disappears as if it crossed a mountain
ridge into thin air. But I can still reach him, braille a message
slowly and put it under his good hand. The over-bed table is
crowded. What can I place in reach, in touch? He doesn't ask,
not even for a drink. I think for him. Could almost believe I
breathe for him like a child. Who will do it for him if not me?

Jill Bamber

Flow-Writing is one of the most useful writing tools we
know. We've both found it invaluable when we've wanted
to explore any theme, personal or otherwise, and to follow
through possibilities before starting a poem. Also if we are

stuck during a piece of writing we find it helpful to take a line or sentence from the material and start Flow-Writing. This method almost always opens up new directions and new images. When we've attended writing groups run by others or ourselves and practised the technique, unexpected, central or interesting material has often come up which has led to further writing. At our writing workshops people are always excited by the possibilities Flow-Writing offers if they haven't come across it before and we know many other writers who make use of it. We've also found that the more we practise it the more it yields.

Clustering

Clustering, like Flow-Writing, is extremely useful as a technique for uncovering interesting subject-matter. Here a word or a phrase is given and the unconscious takes over. But whereas in Flow-Writing you attempt to put down on paper as much as you can of the ideas and feelings presented to you, in Clustering you impose a kind of half-way discipline on yourself. You pluck from the flux further words or phrases related to the given one, and it may well be that these lead in different, even opposing, directions, so that on the page a Cluster rather than a line of words appears. A Cluster is a map of possibilities, a kind of shorthand guide to the contents of your psyche, rather than a single chain of associations.

The technique as we practise it has a clear counterpart in the device of 'Brainstorming' used in lecture-halls, where the teacher calls for contributions on a topic from the assembled students. Clustering is a wider form of brainstorming, not limited to ideas – feelings, sensations, memories, associations are equally important. Once you have drawn your Cluster you then choose the aspect or aspects you wish to feature in your piece of writing. It is not necessary to incorporate the specific words or phrases used in the Cluster.

After you have been practising Clustering for a while you

instinctively appreciate when you have sufficient material to enable you to make a decision about the direction in which your piece might go. For the purposes of the first two exercises we shall suggest a time limit of five minutes for the Clustering and hope that this works for you. You may wish to take up to ten minutes for subsequent Clusters. You will probably need about fifteen minutes for the related pieces of writing.

EXERCISE 12

Juanita Woolliscroft was given the phrase 'Letting Go' to work with, and here are the Cluster and piece of writing that she came up with:

Retirement – letting go of the past, loss of familiar faces, security, old routines, afraid to move on – like a kite stuck in a tree – if only a strong wind would come and blow it away so that it could soar upwards, free to roam wherever the wind takes it, into the unknown future. Possessions, people, a house, a job, security – we need them to give us a feeling of security but at a stroke they can all be taken away – by theft, by fire, by death. Buddhist idea of non-attachment. We have only ourselves, we are born alone, must die alone. All we need is courage to face the unknown future.

Now for your first Cluster try one of the following: 'need', 'confusion', 'surviving', 'lost', 'deception', 'happiness', 'sadness', 'hanging on', 'in at the deep end'.

EXERCISE 13

We come now to some more abstract words. Angela Harker started with the word ANGLE. At first glance her response may appear surprising. Nevertheless her Cluster led to the short piece which follows:

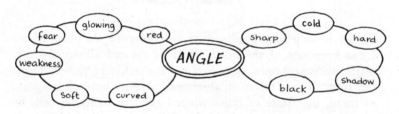

My experience of emotion has always been angular, never curved or soft. I have hidden in the shadows of fear, rejection. Cold, hard – steel, black and grey; never deep red, never glowing. A fear of weakness – hide feelings in dark colours, sharp angles; it keeps them at arm's length. The sharp corners, elbows, knees, are hard to get close to. Soft colours mean weakness – mustn't show.

For your own Cluster see what is called to mind by one of the following: 'corner', 'circle', 'under', 'direction', 'obstruction', 'bridge', 'free-flow', 'weight', 'height'.

EXERCISE 14

You are ready now for a more elaborate piece of Clustering. Ann Sheasby was given the word SILENCE to Cluster. This was the result:

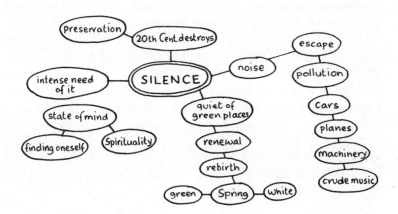

Silence is something I am always searching for – a place where I can keep out of the noise which is created all around me: traffic, radios, phones, amplified music, machinery, raised voices. But silence is more than an absence of invasive noise. It is a state of mind, that state of quiet when I am free to think, feel, be myself. I can touch and hold this silence, its cool inside an old church on a hot day, feel its presence among tall trees in ancient woods, walk through it in the long grass of a water meadow. In this kind of silence I can speak to myself, feel my identity. In this silence I am at my most creative, whether I am conscious of images and ideas or not. I am renewed and able to stay with myself when I return to the rush of noise.

Now use one of the following words for your Cluster: 'separation', 'communication', 'possibility', 'sympathy', 'age', 'colour', 'race', 'class', 'gender'.

EXERCISE 15

Now for some large-scale Clustering. Allow yourself plenty of time for this exercise. But first look at these two examples. The first, based on the word MIRROR, is a really elaborate example of a Cluster, yet the subsequent poem is short and to the point. The second Cluster came from the word DOOR and here a Cluster of modest proportions led to a complex piece of writing. There were so many leads to follow that the writer, who was a prisoner and wishes to remain anonymous, decided to use a format which incorporates as many approaches as possible. John had shown him the Wallace Stevens poem 'Thirteen Ways of Looking at a Blackbird' (to be found in his *Collected Poems*), where each tiny section presents a different aspect of the theme, and the whole is more than the sum of its parts. We print nine sections of the resulting poem in example two.

Example One

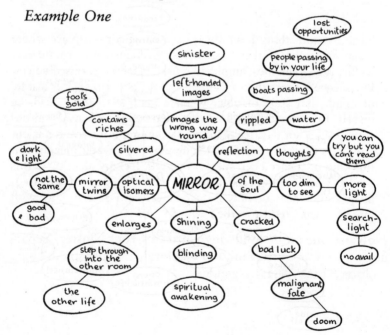

There's something sinister about mirrors
the reflection that isn't you
the not-quite identical twin
left-handed, opposite,
thinking thoughts you wouldn't dare
but still smiling
trying to look normal.
And if you try to find him
to step through the invisible barrier
he slips away
leaving you shattered
dogged by fate
for years to come.

Tony Turner

Example Two

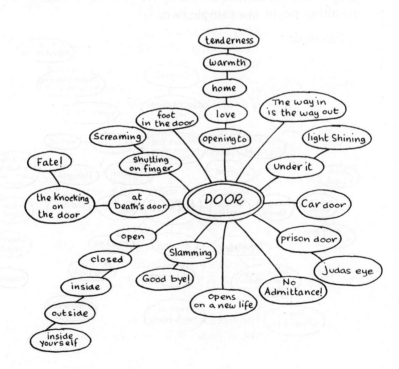

Nine Ways of Looking at Doors

1
Doors opening and closing,
Leaving you inside or outside,
Shut in or shut out.

2
The door that shut on your fingers
When you were two was the first
Lesson on the nature of doors.

3
A sliver of light shining
Under the door that beckoned
You on barefoot to keep
A rendezvous with love.

4
The foot in the door
After your money or
Your soul, a cut-price
Salvation.

5
A door slamming in the night
... 'And don't come back!' ...
Angry feet descending, a woman
Left weeping.

6
The door that shuts within you
As tight-lipped you walk away.

7
The door that opens slowly
When uninvited Death walks in
Asking 'Are you ready?'

8
The steel-faced Judas-eyed door
You cannot open from the inside.

9
The sunshine that explodes
Through the open door
As you walk out
Into a new morning.

Now here are your words to take inspiration from: 'window',
'photograph', 'room', 'knife', 'letter', 'tree', 'river', 'garden',
'underground'.

EXERCISE 16

So far we have used mainly single words as a starting-point.
Here are some phrases to start you off: 'locked out', 'walking
tall', 'might have been', 'head in the clouds', 'keeping in
touch', 'out of bounds', 'in deep', 'living in the past'.

EXERCISE 17

For your final attempt (though we hope that you are hooked
and will go on Clustering through the book and afterwards!)
we suggest you set your own time-limits and provide your
own word or phrase. But we would also like you to attempt
a Double Cluster – that means from your first Cluster you
should select a word or phrase on which to do a second one.
You can base your subsequent piece of writing on the
material thrown up by both Clusters. You will have begun
to realize that Clustering is self-generating and you could go
on Clustering till you have a page, a chapter, even a book!

Modelling

We come now to a technique which might be found contro-
versial, based as it is upon literature rather than life.
However, we feel that it is perfectly legitimate for us to allow
other writings to influence us directly, and believe from our
own experience that this can be a powerfully effective
method so long as the real object of the exercise is never
forgotten: it is just another way of tapping into experience.
Otherwise, we would readily agree that the result will be
pale pastiche, and of no value to anyone. The appeal here is
to the subconscious; tone, rhythm and form can show us
possibilities we might not otherwise have recognized, and
release perceptions that might have remained hidden.

Many writers have attested to the value of strict forms as
a spur to composition. Peter Abbs has written an autobiography entirely in sonnets. He had first of all to accustom his
mind to the length and patterning involved:

> In time, the form became a kind of mould in which the unpredict-
> able flow of experience could be caught, cooled, lifted up and
> made palpable. On a number of occasions I would wake up in
> the morning to find words running through my mind; I would
> scribble them down and find, to my amazement, they were
> sonnet-like utterances, often in fourteen lines and in a rough
> iambic pentameter.

We are not suggesting that you set yourself such difficult tasks as the sonnet, the villanelle or the sestina, only attempting to demonstrate the release that such challenges can represent to the writer. Our proposal is a less forbidding one, though in a sense bolder than this, because it involves making use of what has already been written.

Such an activity is common in other art-forms. Pat B Allen, for example, in her book *Art is a Way of Knowing* says:

> I copy paintings of great artists. When I copy an obscure Picasso painting of a cherry tomato plant growing out of a can, I put down paints in ways I don't know how to. These strokes are fresh and free, as if I am dancing with Picasso and letting him lead. It feels safe, the way tracing a picture is to a fearful child.

Being led by the hand in this way by another writer can be disinhibiting and lead to valuable discoveries both about yourself and about your capacities for expression.

EXERCISE 18

The simplest example of Modelling is Patterning, and we introduced this technique in Part One.

There we employed a list to make a piece of writing. To make this pattern more complicated why not introduce the principle of opposition or contrast into it? That is what Edwin Morgan has done in his poem 'A View of Things'. You can read this piece slowly to puzzle out some of the references, laugh at some of the jokes, ponder some of the profundities. Or you can read it fast and rejoice in what Louis MacNeice called 'the drunkenness of things being various'. Here is the last third of the poem:

what I love about Hank is his string vest
what I hate about the twins is their three gloves
what I love about Mabel is her teeter
what I hate about gooseberries is their look, feel, smell and taste
what I love about the world is its shape

what I hate about a gun is its lock, stock and barrel
what I love about bacon-and-eggs is its predictability
what I hate about derelict buildings is their reluctance to
   disintegrate
what I love about a cloud is its unpredictability
what I hate about you, chum, is your china
what I love about many waters is their inability to quench love

Most people can write for several minutes offering their own likes and dislikes in this format, and the liveliness and variety of Morgan's own examples provide a spur. Give yourself a time-limit of ten minutes and write as spontaneously as you can. Then select the best to form a short poem on the page. As a variation you might like to try writing down likes and dislikes in pairs on the same subject. You are almost certain to find that you have written down one or two really surprising things whichever exercise you try. One of our students could not get over having thought up the following:

what I hate about downpours is their penetration
what I love about a cloud is its tears grow ears of corn

You may find that one of your own lines suggests another piece of writing. The last line in 'A View of Things', for instance, surely has the makings of a further exploration for the poet?

EXERCISE 19

A further development of the 'list' type of poem is where all the observations share the same subject. Here is the opening of Jonathan Davidson's poem 'The Living Room':

The room we argued over Scrabble in,
the room we stayed in when we were ill,
the room we were exiled to, the room
we were banished from for being bad,
the room they hit the roof in, the room
they said we could do as we wished in,

the room they broke the news to us in,
the room we broke the news to them in,
the room we all burst out of in, through
the down-at-heel patio door, into
the knee-deep garden that warm, mild spring,
the room we all went into in winter,
the room we left last when we left, the room
we went to first when we got back.

Through the accumulation of personal details the writer
is really coming to grips with 'the living room' – that formative crucible of family life – and the repetitions help him
to build up a head of steam. Choose a room of your own to
make a list-poem out of. Again, ten minutes should suffice
to provide you with the material from which you can make
a selection for the finished piece. Then try with an object
such as a coat or a tree, or a person whom you like or dislike
especially.

EXERCISE 20

You are now ready to take off into a poem with a more
complex structure. Here is 'Not By This Fire' by Keith
Spencer:

There will be no kindling
to chop for this grate,
no boots steaming in this hearth,
no washing to hang from this mantelpiece,
no hands rubbing flame into chapped skin
not by this fire

the ovens are cold,
there will be no fish-pie this Friday,
no bread to dip into potato broth,
or mop up egg at breakfast
there will be no more rainwater baths
not by this fire

> he will not strip to the waist
> or slip off his braces
> she will not kneel
> to untie his frozen laces
> no, not by this fire
> will he ever roll out his plug again
> or burn in a new briar

This is a poem built from negatives and from convincing domestic details. It is built around the motifs of 'there will be no' and 'not by this'. Read and re-read the poem until its rhythms and repetitions have become imprinted on your subconscious. Now cover it up, choose your own subject and write under the stylistic influence that you have absorbed. You will almost certainly find that the mood of 'Not By This Fire' has been reproduced, and some of its patternings may have got into the poem too, but the piece will have an individual quality as well. Here is the poem John completed in a workshop:

Death of an Old Woman

> There will be no love
> to catch at the breath,
> like climbing the stairs too fast.
>
> There will be no hate
> to boil up in saucepans
> and overspill the stove.
>
> There will be no tears
> to squeeze out at day's end,
> like an old mop in the sink.
>
> Scrubbed like her kitchen bowl,
> she is laid out stark
> in the front parlour's dark.

This is shorter than the original, and only uses one of the repeated phrases, but it similarly employs homely details, and in its very brevity has a character of its own.

EXERCISE 21

Now for a really challenging example: a poem that employs both elaborate Patternings in the form of repetitions of lines and constructions, and that is bound together by an extended metaphor. It also attempts a much deeper exploration of personality. The piece is 'Dream Play' by Dorothy Nimmo:

> I know there's something I must do today.
> It's half-an-hour before curtain rise,
> what is my part in this and what's the play?
> There is a smell of greasepaint, dust and size.
>
> It's half-an-hour before curtain rise, –
> this is the dressing room I know is mine.
> There is a smell of greasepaint, dust and size –
> for God's sake tell me, what's the opening line?
>
> This is the dressing room I know is mine –
> when they begin I'll recognize my cue.
> You're on! they whisper and face the light.
> Who am I? What am I supposed to do?
>
> When they begin I'll recognize my cue.
> You're on! they whisper and I face the light.
> Who am I? What am I supposed to do?
> Forgive me, Mother. Have I got that right?
>
> You're on! they whisper and I face the light.
> I say the line that they expect from me,
> Forgive me, Mother. Have I got that right?
> Was it the daughter that I had to be?
>
> I say the line that they expect from me.
> My voice is strangled. I'm awake. I shout
> It was the daughter that I had to be
> and I can't do it. You must write me out.
>
> My voice is strangled. I'm awake. I shout
> I know there's something I must do today
> and I can't do it. You must write me out.
> It's not my part and this is not my play.

Again we suggest a number of readings, perhaps aloud, will serve to establish the musical structure of the piece in your mind, and will also increase your awareness of the way the imagery works to complement the sounds and create a profound impression of personality-flux. It may be that no such overarching idea of your own presents itself when you start to write. If so, don't worry, let the formal scheme imprinted upon your imagination take you where it chooses.

Example One

Struggling

The day is fine, the sun shines bright outside
but I'm in here and struggling with each line,
the road is clear and I'd enjoy a ride
I wonder if this voice I hear is mine?

But I'm in here and struggling with each line
the words come out and empty on the page.
I wonder if this voice I hear is mine
or echoes of an oriental sage?

The words come out and empty on the page –
the dredgings from a subterranean well?
or echoes from an oriental sage?
and am I lost within a wizard's spell?

These dredgings from a subterranean well –
could they be lures to turn me from the way?
or am I lost within a wizard's spell?
and is this really work or merely play?

Could they be lures to turn me from the way?
The road is clear and I'd enjoy a ride.
And is this really work or merely play?
The day is fine, the sun shines bright outside.

                                        Tony Turner

Example Two

'When I am Free from the Prisoner's Fate'

When I am free from the prisoner's fate
I'm going to drink tea fresh from the pot.
When I am released from this caught-up state
There will be no more remembering what should be forgot.

When I am free from the prisoner's fate
I'm going to dance and sing for a day.
When I am released from this caught-up state
I'll no longer act as if in a play.

When I am free from the prisoner's fate
I'm going to walk in the room with no shoes.
When I am released from this caught-up state
There will be no more time to win or lose.

When I am free from the prisoner's fate
I will place your flowers in a porcelain vase.
When I am released from this caught-up state
I will circle the moon and fly to the stars.

When I am released from the prisoner's fate
... I'm going to buy ANDREX toilet paper!!!

Example Three

Who's That?

Who's that? she asks, as someone passes through.
That's Sue, I say, the one who cares for you.
Oh! Is that Sue? ... I want a cup of tea.
Tea-time is soon – it's only half-past three.

When's tea-time? Is it time for you to go?
No, mother, I've just come ... Oh, don't you know,
it's such a lovely day we could go out.
No! ... Don't leave me ... Did I hear a shout?

I'm hungry. Have you brought something to eat?
I'll peel a pear. I know you like a treat.
Another piece. And more, and more and more.
A cup of tea will come at half-past-four.

You're slipping down. Here, let me shift you, dear.
Hold on tight. It's all right. I'm right here.
I'll put this rose in water by your chair.
Perhaps it will remind when I'm not there.

It's time for me to go. Give me a kiss.
I'll come again on Sunday. Here, take this.
Maria, will you let me out? I'll go
before the held-back tears begin to flow.

Joy Winterbottom

Each of these poems was written in a workshop. We are
giving you three examples in order to demonstrate the variety
that is possible when taking another piece of writing as a
formal model.

The first sticks closely to the original though its tone is
much lighter. The second was written by a woman in prison.
It does not have the richness of the original, and it adopts a
more easygoing Patterning, but it does have fantasy and
humour and served its purpose for the author of providing
a satisfying outlet for her longings. The last is again formally
exact, and the echoing structure mirrors the conversational
patterns set up by mother and daughter in a poignant way.

If you find Modelling a stimulating way of unearthing new
subject-matter you will easily be able to supply yourself with
some new Models by leafing through a good anthology of
poetry.

Tapping into Memory

Memory is an essential part of ourselves. Without it we cannot find our bearings in time and place, make connections with other people, understand ourselves. In *The Man Who Mistook His Wife for a Hat*, Oliver Sacks writes about the predicament of 'the lost mariner', a middle-aged man stranded in life because he could not remember beyond his nineteenth year. John's work with people suffering from dementia reveals over and over again their acute sense of loss because of the fragmentation of their memories.

Some people are distressed because they can remember very little about their childhood. In an article about writing autobiography Peter Abbs says: 'Much of my early life seems lost in a kind of permanent winter drizzle. I am envious of those who can enter their childhood like a lit landscape.' He comes to the conclusion that his commitment to the genre of autobiography is a kind of compensation for a sluggish memory. A member of a writing group, who could remember nothing of her first six years, told Myra: 'In order to know myself I feel I must make up my childhood.'

The experience of childhood is so potent it is not surprising that it is often the source of literature: Wordsworth's poem *The Prelude*, the early chapters of Charlotte Bronte's *Jane Eyre*, Donald Atkinson's long poem *A Sleep of Drowned*

Fathers and so on. In 'Missing Locks' Colin Rowbotham remembers the pleasure of fingering a 'metal nest' of keys:

> A butterfly windup one, tiny gun barrels
> For bureaux and watches,
> A rustroughened, jigsawtoothed
> Giant from someone's backdoor.

Our lives are so shaped by childhood that recalling this kind of detail, the events and feelings round it, must be an important element in self-discovery through writing. Almost any of the techniques described in this book could set off memories, but because memory is so crucial we are including this section to suggest some ways of tapping directly both into childhood and other areas of the past.

An old diary or letters written by you or to you may be very important in offering you information about a precise time in your past. If you have this kind of material the first thing you might want to do is to write and Flow-Write about events and feelings it reminds you of. You may also want to read these records when you are doing the following exercises. If you have no material of this kind to refer to it doesn't matter. The exercises will spark off details, situations, episodes and feelings, some of which you may not have thought about for a long time.

EXERCISE 22

Look round your home and collect a few objects that are connected with your past. These might be items of clothing, jewellery, ornaments, books, paintings, etc, that you have owned for a long time or were maybe passed on to you by your parents, grandparents or friends. Choose one that has special significance for you. Begin by describing it in detail: size, shape, colours, texture, smell, weight. Then write as much as you can about any or all of the following: where it was kept, any events or people it reminds you of, the period of your life you associate it with, your feelings then, the feelings the object triggers off now.

EXERCISE 23

Now try a variation of the first exercise by making a list of objects you remember from different times in your past but no longer have. Search your mind for 'key' possessions. It doesn't matter if you cannot remember them in great detail. Here are some possibilities: your first bicycle, your desk at school when you were eight, a cupboard you hid in, a fireplace, party clothes, a matchbox in which you kept a caterpillar, a letter from someone important, a ring, the hopeless kitchenette in the first flat you lived in, etc. Write for seven minutes or longer about two of these.

Example

My Blue Glass Fox Head

My brother gave it to me at the end of a school holiday, my second term away from home – he knew how I feared it. It was a blue glass fox head that might have fallen off a charm bracelet, or been won at a fair. You could hold it up to the light so that the white painted eyes blurred and all you could see was blue. 'For luck,' he said. I kept it on the shelf beside my bed, my only shelf. This was regularly gone through by Matron Windsor. But she was kind. She'd confiscate other things. 'What's this on your sheets?' she said one day. 'Brown grains?' She knew I was too young for periods – knew very well that they must have come from a precious tin of ovaltine, eaten under the bedclothes because I was ravenous. 'Hand it over,' she said. And I did. But one day the blue glass fox head went from its place under the few hair grips my mother had sent back with me. I suspected no one. I guess I daren't. Wondering was dangerous. I searched obsessively and never really gave up hope.

Juliette Carter

EXERCISE 24

Now try using photographs as triggers. These might be old photographs of yourself or others which summon up situations or events, yourself in your first class at school, yourself outside a home you left when you were very young, a family pet you loved, a photograph of a parent or sibling or family friend, a group sitting outside a tent, your first boyfriend/girlfriend, yourself at work, on a mountain, etc. Postcards or photographs of the kind of places you knew or visited in the past, or of activities you enjoyed as a child, or which include vehicles, machines or other objects you associate with your past may be equally effective triggers. Begin by describing the photograph and the person/people in it in detail and then everything you remember about yourself at this time – the sort of things you did, wore, who you knew, what you felt, incidents relating to that time. One memory is very likely to set off others you want to write about.

Example

I am looking at the camera, waiting for Grandpa to call 'Cheese' from underneath the black cloth. He's standing on the balcony with the camera pointing downwards on us, his face and shoulders hidden. I can hear the scrape of the fresh glass plate inserted into the camera [. . .] And oh, it's so hot, I want to shout: 'Hurry up Grandpa, I want to go inside for a glass of cold water' [. . .]

A bee is making its way, busily touching the blossom. It buzzes near Aunt and starts to explore the silk flowers of her hat. I can feel my stomach go taut because I'm scared of bees. I wiggle my head, trying to keep the movements small because Aunt will be cross. I can hear the bee-buzz louder in my right ear and imagine its furry bumbleness louder in my right ear. It crawls from my hat to my hair. Maybe it will tunnel deep into my ear, sting my brain and I'll die. The thought brings me out in shivery goosebumps. The cold is like Grandma's icebox, cold as the big block of ice at the top with its metal pick to stab off pieces of ice for drinks or to put into Aunt's handkerchief for a headache. I imagine a searing pain, the bee sting stabbing like the ice pick. The sharp tip hurts in my head, blows up into an enormous pain till I can't bear it any more and scream: 'Mummy, mummy!' the way I did when I was three and had those awful nightmares. There's a zizzy feeling, prickles in my fingers and toes and a sudden blackness with whorls of light.

When I come to Aunt is leaning over me, her ear next to my heart and her fat hot fingers loosening the buttons at the collar of my dress.

Ann Griswold

This vividly realized piece was triggered by a postcard which was a photograph of people sitting stiffly in the sun, posing for the camera. It is an interesting mixture of fact and fiction. Ann comments that Grandpa taking the photograph and the icebox were real but that the incident with the bee is imagined. However, 'the bee' is exactly in line with her child-hood fears and fantasies. This 'memory' is an excellent example of how useful fiction can be in helping to re-create fully the way one felt as a child – the whole texture of one's past – and this approach is likely to be helpful to those who find it difficult to recall the detail of childhood.

EXERCISE 25

Now try using place as a trigger. Choose a room in a house or flat where you lived, part of a garden, a road, view, shop, place of work, beach, playing field, piece of waste ground, station you've often travelled from, anywhere that you associate with a particular time in your past. Visualize it as fully as you can. Begin by describing it and then Flow-Write about the memories the place sets off.

Examples

In the big basement room a dresser went from floor to ceiling; there were open shelves for the white plates with blue rims.

Everything was big and mostly out of my reach. Both the store cupboard and the toy cupboard had wooden shelves going far back. I had to climb on the shelves in order to reach my toys and books.

The room was dominated by a full size billiard table. There had been four boys in my mother's family. Two had died before they reached thirty. Their violins still hung on the wall of the toy cupboard. Another was the black sheep and was never mentioned, and the other bachelor brother owned this house. In my childhood the billiard table was covered by a wooden top. The shiny balls still hung in string bags under the table. I used to feel their smooth shiny surfaces and bang them together to make a satisfying click.

I remember standing by the open door of the toy cupboard with a new china doll I had been given that day. I lifted her to give her a ride on my shoulders as my daddy used to do to me but she fell to the floor and broke.

Bernadette Cronin

The room didn't grab me. I loved the view beyond: the lights. I'd learned the special word for the middle one's colour and the special word for what it meant: caution. The cars obeyed their power. Excitement, power, happiness – that was what it meant to be grown-up, not so weak I could hardly push the wheelbarrow and never had more than 10p.

What on earth went on in banks? What was it like to stay up late? Really late. After 10. Once, Kim the *au pair* had spirited me through Worthing at that time and I saw the lights – incredible. But in the end she stuffed me back in bed, the curtains drawn.

When I wasn't daring enough to pull their purple back, I looked at my Womble posters: especially Tobermory who looked like Paddington and reminded me of me: afraid, into jokes, always making mistakes mistakes mistakes. But I felt safe in the room except for nightmares; plus now and then a power drill roared, a blackbird slammed the glass.

David Wilson

EXERCISE 26

The people who have been important in your life may have cropped up already in pieces of writing you have done but this is an opportunity to begin to focus on people who have mattered to you in the past. Choose two you would like to write a few paragraphs about. There are different ways to tackle this.

1 It may be clear to you immediately that you want to write about a person for a particular reason – a teacher because he or she had an important influence on what you studied and your later career, a grandparent you were very close to, someone who helped you through a crisis, a friend you've helped, someone you worked with every day for a year, etc. In this case you might want to concentrate on showing the part your chosen person has played in your life. If he/she belonged to your early childhood you may only have a few memories and want to record everything you can remember.

2 If your relationship with the person you are writing about had a definite shape – an affair, a friendship that was supportive in your last two years at school, a rivalry or a set-up in which you were victimized until you stood up for yourself and so on – you may find it best to write a narrative.

3 If you are not quite sure where you want to begin or how to tackle writing about the person you've chosen, write down the first sentence about him or her that comes into your mind, then Flow-Write for seven minutes or so. When you stop, underline phrases or sentences which suggest ideas for writing more fully, arrange them in order, then use them as guidelines to develop your piece. Alternatively, write down the person's name and use the Clustering technique to help you sort out what you most want to write.

Here are Isobel Thrilling's memories of an aunt who was significant to her.

> During the war, at the age of four, I was evacuated to her house. Although she was a relative I had never met her before. The images that come are marshmallow, pink and white cushions, a large lady. She is showing me the evening dress she will wear to a big Christmas dance. It is many layers of black net scattered with silver sequins and makes me think of the night sky and stars. She has yellow hair and I imagine it arranged on top of her head like the moon. She is stroking the dress tenderly and I know (though I couldn't have put it into words) this action makes her vulnerable in some way.
>
> Another piece of film forms. I am hovering near the kitchen door where my aunt is baking. The smell of the steam rising from a tray of hot jam tarts is as potent as the smoke of a genie and just as magical [. . .]
>
> The final image is much more traumatic. My mother and father have come unexpectedly to take me home. When I see them I burst out sobbing, run through the back door, down the path and into the street. I fall. My knee bleeds profusely. My uncle picks me up and hands me into the large, comforting arms of my aunt but I know I must leave. I see my mother's face. She does not speak.

EXERCISE 27

Sometimes sense impressions – smells, sounds, textures, tastes, sights – take us back to the past more powerfully than anything else. Make a list of smells that bring back your childhood or some time in your past. Here are some possibilities: bonfire smoke, lavender, the smell of washing drying on a line, cow dung, soot, cocoa, chips, friar's balsam, sweat, Dettol, petrol, violets. Describe one of the smell memories and Flow-Write about what it conjures up. Then explore the other senses in the same way. When thinking about sounds don't forget to include pieces of music and when listing textures think about the feel of clothes you remember.

Example

List of Tastes

The salt roughness of sea on the lips
melting richness of licked chocolate
smooth bright sweetness of jelly
the awful lumpiness of porridge
the crispiness of roast potatoes
the tart and sweetness of raspberries

I hated porridge anyway, the scum on the top, the obscene thickness with lumps, the loathsome milkiness, the smell – and then in hospital, terrified, throat hurting, nurses prickly, my mother allowed in for such a short time, the total misery of porridge without even the disguise of golden syrup but with salt – trying to force it down, the nurse looming, her face full of threat, when I just couldn't, couldn't.

Ben Williams

EXERCISE 28

Focusing on particular feelings often triggers off memories. Once in a writing workshop Myra asked everyone to write about fear and half the group wrote about memories of being bullied. Choose two or three feelings and write about the memories they set off. Here are some possibilities: disappointment, curiosity, hope, fear, anger, joy, powerlessness, excitement, panic, love, jealousy, hate, determination, humiliation.

EXERCISE 29

Similarly, exploring key experiences or certain kinds of experience will bring the past flooding back. Pick two which immediately set off memories and spend ten minutes or more narrating/Flow-Writing about them. Here are some ideas: your first realization of death, your first day at school, playing truant from school, ill-treating an animal, keeping a secret, hiding, telling lies, disobeying, being bullied, teasing someone, being excluded either as a child or later, exploring places, imaginary worlds, cruelty, first seeing a member of the opposite sex (or the same sex) naked, puberty, quarrels in the family, parents separating, falling in love, leaving home, an incident in which you felt there was prejudice against you, a success, a failure, a loss, a celebration.

Example

Disobedience

I saw it as an act of gross disobedience to keep back a penny of my bus money and then get off the bus two stops early but I wanted to keep in with Meg Dewar so I allowed her to persuade me and then I followed her into the sweet shop on the promenade above the rocky shore and used my saved penny to buy sherbet – just like she did. The sherbet grazed my throat. I hated it. I hated the whole escapade and as we walked along the road the enormity of my crime grew. What excuse could I give my mother for mis-spending my bus money, for being late home? Terrified, I asked Meg. 'I'll come home with you and explain you lost some of your money.' We climbed the hill towards her house where she stopped off to tell her mother she was coming home with me. Her mother wasn't interested, sent her out on an errand. 'I'll come in a wee while,' Meg promised. I waited desperately at the foot of the steps that led to the steep road up to my house. I could think of nothing but the mountain of my mother's anger. It began to get dark. A policeman came along and asked me why I was standing there. I mumbled that I was waiting for my friend. He told me to go home. Frightened, I obeyed. I was crying when I reached our house. I think I poured out the truth. I can't remember what my mother said, only my surprise that her anger was nothing like as great as I had imagined it would be and my relief as the huge fear inside me let go.

Maureen Mackay

EXERCISE 30

Now choose an experience you want to write about which doesn't immediately bring up a clear memory. It may be from the list or something else you think of. Use the Clustering technique to help you identify what you'd like to write. Then write for ten minutes or more.

Later, particularly if you decide to write your autobiography, you will probably want to come back to this section and do more tapping into memory.

Image Explorations

Many of the influences, feelings, attitudes, beliefs, that shape us are so interwoven, so deeply ingrained it is difficult to identify and separate them. In any case some would be overwhelming or painful if they were looked at head-on, and to try to pick them out before they surfaced naturally might be counter-productive. As well as tapping directly into our feelings, thoughts and memories we believe it is valuable to explore indirectly, to offer 'keys' which will allow the imagination to choose what doors it opens, what paths it takes.

One such key is dream, which has a section to itself. Another is Image Exploration. By offering metaphors, symbols, story or fantasy beginnings we hope you will enjoy travelling your inner world freely, that you will make exciting discoveries, find forgotten treasure, make new connections with rich, significant, difficult, inexplicable experiences without necessarily feeling you must label or explain them.

We suggest you try two of the image journeys offered here. In these exercises you may mix fact and fiction in any way you like as long as you remain truthful to your vision and feelings.

EXERCISE 31: CROSSROADS

You are walking by yourself, maybe have been walking for a long time. Picture your surroundings, what you are carrying, how hard or easy the journey has been, how you are feeling. Describe all this.

You come to a crossroads. You have a choice of two different ways forward. They are very different from one another. There is no obvious way of deciding which direction to take. Describe the different routes. What is your reaction to them? Write about what you do, what happens, how you feel.

Example

I am burdened – a suitcase in my right hand, a bag slung over my right arm – a small but heavy back-pack, a plastic carrier in my left hand. I'm lopsided. Stones dig into my feet. A low sun blinds me as I struggle upwards. A little further and the sun is obscured behind a hill and I arrive at a crossroads. To my left is a narrow pathway even steeper than that I have just climbed. Another to my right climbs again but less steeply and in front a flat path appears to go on for ever. Fear knits my stomach. I become aware of an old man. He touches my right elbow and looks at me as if to say: 'Which way shall we go?' I choose the slope to the right – uphill again but gentler, and in some strange way inviting. The path is grassy and with bushes on either side. Later a tunnel of trees shelters us from the noon sun. In the late afternoon out on the bare mountainside the sun begins to set. I watch the colours and my companion comes to stand behind me. He is there yet not there. He has become part of me.

Sue Parker

EXERCISE 32: AN ENCOUNTER

You enter a building or compartment and sit down. You might be in a waiting room, hotel lobby, train, your kitchen, a café, an attic, a summerhouse, etc. Write about your surroundings, why you are there and how you are feeling.

Someone comes and sits beside or near you. It might be someone you know or a stranger. You can see that this person is feeling very strongly about something – excited, worried or upset, for example. What do you have to say to this person and what might he/she say to you? How do things develop between you? Write about this.

EXERCISE 33: WATER

You are walking through a place where the going is difficult and you have little or no view. Write about this.

Suddenly everything opens out and you come upon water. It may be the sea, a lake, a pool, a waterfall, etc. What you see or what happens by the water changes your feelings. Write about all this. Include a description of the water and anything you can see on or beneath its surface. Show how your feelings change.

Example

Everywhere thick branches obstructing and knotty twigs. The path I was on has disappeared. The wood is pulling me into its trap. I blunder forward. 'You're a ninny, not a man!' The voice in my head is sharper than the spiteful thorns. Suddenly there is space ahead, sunlight in a speedwell-blue sky. I break through brambles and find myself at the edge of water stretching as far as I can see – a lake of silence that brings the sky to my feet. I am free of something I cannot put into words. On the surface: glimmers of movement and in the distance a single bird is swimming. I stand for a long time staring at the delicate thread of its neck.

Mark Peterson

EXERCISE 34: THE SAFE PLACE

You are afraid of someone or something or your fear may
be undefinable. You are searching for a safe place and come
upon a cubby hole, bed, niche or other place of refuge and
go into it. Describe this.

Gradually you relax. The hideaway reminds you of places
or maybe people who've made you feel safe and comfortable
in the past or the safety you are experiencing may be something you have long wanted and never before found. Write
about your feelings.

Example

I ran, panicking, to the art gallery, my usual place of refuge. No
one seemed to be following me as they had done on previous
occasions I'd run out of the ward. Disregarding the permanent
display of staid Victorian landscapes and wilder Augustus Johns,
I entered the special exhibition room. I felt afraid, yet what of?
It was more than a fear of discovery, of capture, of return. It
was a fear which permeated everything, every breath breathed
was clouded with fear like absinthe in a glass. What I saw
hanging on the walls confounded me. Each painting depicted an
eye slashed with a razor blade, red and staring and menacing.
Terrified, I moved hypnotically round the room.

I went out into the street, in and out of the shops; everything
was red, bloody and frightening. Eventually I made my way to
the Winter Gardens, a series of huge greenhouses in the park
[. . .] a refuge not only because of their cosy almost stifling
warmth but in the reassurance of living, growing leaves and
flowers, water trickling in little fountains into pools where gold-
fish swam placidly, unaware of my terror and thus comforting.
I sat on a seat [. . .] and slowly began to feel the beginnings of
safety. The warmth, the heavy fragrance, the slow mesmerizing
pooling of fish – perhaps I felt safe because it was like the womb
and like the incubator in which I spent the first few months of
my life.

Jane Harris

EXERCISE 35: NEW BEARINGS

You are in a strange place. You can see buildings, plants, birds, people but nothing looks or sounds familiar. Write about this.

A person (or it could be a group of people) approaches you, speaks to you and offers you something but you can't understand a single word. You very much want to make contact but feel certain you won't be understood.

What do you do? What happens next and how do you feel? Describe all this.

Example

Low flimsy buildings with gardens full of bright bushes, palms and cacti, went the length of the street. There were people everywhere, all various shades of brown. I looked at my arm. It was a sickly white. The air was too hot and smelt of fragrant tea. I felt homesick, horribly alone.

A girl with masses of wonderful thick wavy hair came towards me. She was holding a dish of prickly fruit. Inanely I asked her what the fruit was. Her reply seemed to be in English but I couldn't make out a word of it. I was so disappointed I almost cried. Laughing, she pointed to a table under a blue sunshade. She was stunningly beautiful and there was a generosity about her which I knew I'd been longing for all my life. We sat down.

Mike Simpson

EXERCISE 36: THE WALL

You are standing by a high wall which stretches in both directions as far as you can see. Describe the wall and its effect on you.

You hear a voice on the other side. Do you make contact with someone, find a way over or through the wall? What happens and how does it affect you? Write about this.

Example

> I'm up against it:
> the unyielding haecceity of it,
> I can't penetrate its stubbornness,
> rub my hands on its rough surfaces,
> move along more than a fraction
> of its endless obduracy,
> upright but crabwise,
> hand over hand, searching
>
> for a crack, longing for a fault,
> a green embrasure.
> But my dilemma:
> is it keeping me in
> or keeping me out?
>
> Then a voice, a high-
> pitched calling, almost
> song-like in this brick
> implacability. What is she
> trying to convey,
> that she has found a way
> out or round? The sound
> tantalizes – maybe
> it is there to taunt me
> or provide hope
> in a hopeless situation?
> It enshrines my longing:
> man put me in this place,
> will woman save me from it?
>
> *Steven Forster*

EXERCISE 37: THE BOX

Imagine you are sitting in a place you know very well. You are holding a box on your lap and are keyed up with anticipation because you have a sense that the box's contents are significant. Describe the place where you are sitting, the box and your feelings.

Now imagine yourself opening the box and carefully lifting out what is inside. The object might be something you've seen before or something you've imagined. It might be big or small, exotic or humdrum but it has a strong effect on your feelings. Perhaps you find some special significance in it. Describe the object, your reactions to it, also what you do with it or want to do with it.

EXERCISE 38: THE SEARCH

You are lost in a large, anonymous building which has many floors, corridors and doors. You are looking for someone or something. Who or what is it? Describe the building and your search. At last you hear music on the other side of a door. The sound moves you and you stand very close to the door. How does the music make you feel? What does it make you think of? Do you go into the room? Write about all this.

EXERCISE 39

When you have tried two of these exercises invent an Image Exploration for yourself. Give your imagination free rein and it will lead you to material you want to write about. Here is a list of images which you might find it useful to refer to: fire, a mountain, circles, loops, a river, flying, rocks, eggs, the moon, steps, a tunnel, diving, a bird, a tree, a journey, a clown, blindfold, a skyscraper, a bridge, hands, heart, sky, island, a stone, eyes, a platform, a hothouse, a parade, a judge, a needle, a book, a queen, a king.

If you have enjoyed this technique try it again when you are further on in the book. You may find it valuable to make up an Image Exploration round a subject or feeling you want to explore in detail, e.g. indecision, confusion, fear, making contact with people, needing space, etc.

Letters, Dramatized Scenes, Narratives and Internal Dialogues

An illuminating way of investigating oneself is to write letters, dialogues, dramatized scenes and narratives which address directly confrontations, situations, issues in relationships and other problems that you have been unable, for one reason or another, to explore or face in life. It can also be constructive to write about happenings and confrontations which did take place and develop them differently from the way they actually went. Such exercises offer a channel for releasing feelings which may have been held back for a long time. They also allow one to look closely, and from different perspectives, both at one's own behaviour and that of people one finds or found it difficult to communicate with. This kind of exploration is likely to lead to a deeper understanding of oneself and others. It may also reveal new possibilities for an existing relationship or for future relationships.

Many dialogues between people who are intimate follow set patterns. Each responds in character and the words they speak are only cues to the next stage. Even if one of them tries to vary the pattern, the listener(s) may well force the conversation back on its predictable course, leaving the person who is trying to take the initiative – a teenager with a changing awareness of the world, for example – feeling infuriated or oppressed.

Most conversations are on two levels. Beneath the words that are spoken aloud is an unspoken communication: body language, the tension or understanding of unstated thoughts and feelings, coded messages. This may be much closer to what is really going on between the speakers. In an intimate, harmonious relationship the silent communication adds to the bond. However, there is often a discrepancy between the spoken and the unspoken. It is not unusual for conversations to be exercises in avoiding the issue.

Good writers are adept at indicating this duality. Sometimes they bypass the outer voice altogether. In the play *The Bed*, Jim Cartwright makes the characters, who all share a giant bed, communicate their feelings and thoughts in their 'under voices'. In Virginia Woolf's poetic novel *The Waves* the characters only speak in monologues which come directly from their inner selves. 'Strange Meeting' by Wilfred Owen is a vision in which the poet meets a dead soldier, the enemy he killed yesterday. Much of the poem is the soldier's monologue and his voice is perhaps the voice of all killed soldiers. We also feel that he is Owen's other self, the one who foresaw that he would soon be a victim of the war.

EXERCISE 40

The first technique we'd like you to experiment with is Secret Letters. Choose someone you know or knew well but find/ found it difficult to talk to. It might be a relative or sibling you are in conflict with, a colleague you loathed, someone who undervalues you, who hurt you badly or completely misunderstands you, someone whose attitudes to gender, religion or other matters you hate. Write a letter to this person saying exactly what you dislike about him or her, what you see as the problems in your relationship or how he or she has misunderstood you, etc. The letter is private or 'secret' because it will not, in fact, be seen by the person it is addressed to (or anyone else unless you wish to show it) so you can say exactly what you want to without any sense of restriction. You can also adopt any tone you like, write in as much or as little detail as you want to. There is no need to be fair – use strong language or whatever words come into your head. You may find you can't wait to start your letter but if you find it difficult to let go and be direct with your chosen person try the simple expedient of changing his/her name and see if this removes the sense of restriction. If that doesn't work try writing to an invented person first of all. Then see if you can address a real one!

Example

Dear Marsha,

It is difficult to know where to begin in this letter, overwhelming to find that I have been given this permission and this page on which to speak to you directly, to tell you what I really feel, really think instead of fending you off as best as I can and then afterwards voicing my rage and hurt to Michael or whichever dear friend will listen.

I can't bear your sanctimonious, superior I-know-best manner or the martyr's role you have taken upon yourself and the games you play round this which I don't want to take part in. Nor can I understand the right you seem to think you have, because you are six years older and my sister, to judge and interfere. I am fed up with your contempt for my pottery which people actually buy. You've made it clear you think my values are wrong – well I hate yours and detest you for assuming you are RIGHT. I wish I had the nerve to tell you to fuck off and get out of my life.

Why, why did you tell poor old Auntie Beth that you and I think she should sell her cottage and go into a residential home? How dare you! You've never discussed this with me. I've now told her what I think – that she should stay put and get helpers to come in. Just for your information she cried with relief.

I could go on listing how you upset, enrage, irritate or bore me but at the end of it all there is the huge sadness that there is no closeness, no past or anything else to enjoy sharing.

Joanna Harding

EXERCISE 41

When you've finished the letter try writing an answer from the recipient if you can and if it seems fruitful, continue the correspondence. Alternatively choose a person you believe has strong views about you and write a letter which expresses his/her attitude to you. Again follow up this letter with your reply.

Imagining yourself as another character in your life is a very potent way of finding out something about his/her motivation, feelings and behaviour. It enables you to see life from the other person's perspective – not your own, however painful your involvement might have been.

Myra found herself using this technique without planning to do so. The first step was talking to her mother, who enjoyed going over her past, and making notes about her mother's childhood and the life of her maternal grandmother. The restrictions of her grandmother's life and the way she treated her mother seemed significant. After her mother's death Myra wrote a sequence of poems about her grandmother and her mother's early life, drawing on the material she'd gathered. While she was working on the poems she felt first of all as if she was her grandmother, then her mother. By the time she had finished she had gained a new understanding of these women. She also felt a sympathy, especially for her mother, that she had not experienced before. (The sequence of poems, 'Mother and Daughter', is in *Crossing Point*.)

EXERCISE 42

The letter technique offers the opportunity to present a complete point of view and then follow it up by presenting another. By using dialogue you can look at interaction, recreate 'the fabric' of a relationship or one of its key moments. Choose a highly-charged relationship you would like to explore. It might involve a particular event or an ongoing situation. Now depict the pattern of conversation that occurs between yourself and the other person or re-create in dialogue the particular incident you want to focus on. Only use the words spoken and set them out in play form. If necessary include stage directions in brackets.

Example

DAUGHTER: You know you never treated me as an adult. You didn't want me to grow up it seemed although I'm not sure you enjoyed having children either, did you?

MOTHER: I wanted you to grow up, of course, but I couldn't see that you have grown up, not the way I understood growing up. You were so changeable, always having a new idea and being so vehement about it, then saying something completely different. Do you feel that was grown up?

DAUGHTER: Yes, they were my ideas, that's what you didn't like about them. Although they changed they were always different to your ideas. You insisted that I was just 'trying to be different'. You couldn't see that I was different.

MOTHER: I don't know what you expected. I did my best. You were a sweet little girl. I brought you up to be a good Christian but people are so selfish.

DAUGHTER: You mean I'm selfish.

MOTHER: Yes, you are selfish. You never thought what effect you were having on me – worrying the life out of me.

DAUGHTER: Should I have thought of the effect on you before living my life?

MOTHER: Why not?

DAUGHTER: Because how can anything get done in the world if people always think about whether they will worry their mothers before they do it?

Liz Houghton

EXERCISE 43

Now see if you can write a fuller scene perhaps with more characters and possibly with some kind of change taking place. Show the different characters' viewpoints in the dialogue. The scene could involve a row, incompatible attitudes, prejudice, lying, harassment, illness, discovery, a breakthrough of some kind, etc. If you like you can transcend reality and make the speakers talk from their inner selves as the play develops. Feel free to re-write and/or develop what actually happened. If appropriate add another scene. If you like this technique try it again with a different incident.

EXERCISE 44

Take another significant, dramatic or complex event/situation from your life, for example the marriage your parents didn't want you to make, the conflict with a neighbour whose son taunts yours, the conflict with your parents or partner over your attitude to money, an explosive work situation, the son who thinks you are a neurotic old man/woman, a conflict with your partner who has a drink problem or expects you to fit in with her/him. This time 'relate' the story from the viewpoint of one of the characters (not yourself). If possible write another version of the same event from a second point of view. This could be someone less directly involved, for example a mother worried about the relationship between her son and his partner. Finally, and with any new insights you have gained, write about the incident from your own viewpoint.

EXERCISE 45

There is one more dialogue technique for self-discovery which we want to introduce in this section. This relates to the 'characters' within yourself and the discussions and arguments which occur in your own mind. We all have a variety of inner voices: the voice that urges one on, the voice that criticizes, the voice that responds to other people's needs, a guilty voice, a voice that pushes away difficulties and so on. Shakespeare's character Hamlet is someone who finds it difficult to come out of his inner world. His soliloquies are full of inner argument and the ghost of his father could be thought of as a dramatic embodiment of a guilty voice speaking inside himself.

Listen out for your inner voices and their conversations. You may already know these very well but if you find it difficult to pick them out try pinpointing a time when you are in two minds about something and see if you can hear the dialogue, argument, browbeating, etc, that is going on in your head. Begin by writing down a few exchanges between the voices you have just recognized or try writing the sort of conversation that often takes place in your head. Here are some possibilities: child and adult, optimist and pessimist, dreamer and realist, adventurous voice and cautious voice, critic and supporter, energetic voice and lazy voice, panicky and calming voice, doubting and hopeful voice.

Example

DOUBTING: What sort of job do you think you'll be able to get after all this time? Okay, you've got experience in catering and community care, but that was years ago, and you never did get any qualifications. It's a lot more competitive out there now.

HOPEFUL: Hold on there – I've got qualities a lot of highly trained people haven't got – strong communication skills, an ability to be flexible, understanding, patience. These things will open a lot of doors.

DOUBTFUL: Employers won't be impressed. After four years looking after the kids (while your wife was training and then out at work) you're completely out of touch. You've lost direction and you're not that

young any more or as agile. You're going to find it
tough – probably have to settle for some menial
cleaning job.

HOPEFUL: You're forgetting the references I've collected over
the years. Not many people can boast testimonials
like those. Chances are I'll be spoilt for choice. As
for losing direction – show me someone who hasn't
at some time in their lives.

Malcolm Bradley

EXERCISE 46

Now try writing a more complex dialogue between two or
maybe more inner voices you want to explore. Begin by
making a list of your inner voices. As well as those already
mentioned it may include some of the following: the inferior
voice, the superior voice, the martyred voice, the deter-
mined voice, the defiant voice, the avoid-confrontation-at-
all-costs voice, the investigating voice, the shrugging-it-off
voice, the understanding voice, the impatient voice, the
anything-for-a-quiet-life voice, the something-will-turn-up
voice, the giving-up voice and so on. Here is John Sandridge's
inner dialogue between what he has labelled as his Wounded
Adult Child voice and his Wicked Step Mother voice which
he describes as the bit in himself which says 'jump'
whenever he gets to the edge of a cliff. He says he likes to
bring the Wicked Step Mother out into the open to prevent
her creeping up on him unawares and hitting him from
behind.

WSM: You're ugly and disgusting and you make me want to
throw up.

WAC: I can't help being fat.

WSM: Fat? You're not fat, you're obscene. You're taller lying
down than you are standing up. I'm ashamed to be seen
with you.

WAC: Can't you ever say anything kind?

WSM: I am being kind. I'm telling you the truth. People laugh at you in the street. Just *look* at yourself.

WAC: That's the problem. I can't. I can't see what's me any more. When I look in the mirror all I see is what you call me. I'm not a person any more. I'm a *thing*.

WSM: You can say that again – a blob. You make me want to puke.

WAC: How can you say that? You're supposed to love me.

WSM: Love! You have to earn love . . .

WAC: Hold on – this isn't about me at all. You can't love yourself so you're turning it onto me. I've carried this stuff around for years and it's not even mine to carry. You think *you're* ugly so you dump it all on me.

EXERCISE 47

As a finale you might like to try writing a scene from your life, first the outer dialogue between yourself and the other person or people involved and then follow this with the inner dialogues which take place inside you during this scene. If you feel like it include the inner dialogues of the other character or characters.

Dreams and Active Imaginings

Almost half of our lives are spent asleep. What is more, that is the half of our lives over which the unconscious mind holds sway, so it would be foolish to neglect it as a source of insights for our greater understanding of the self, as well as an inexhaustible well-spring for writing. Dreaming is the language which the unconscious uses for self-communing. Its vocabulary is one of symbols, and in our quest for self-discovery we need to approach dreams with humility and open-mindedness. Their force comes from their being poised on a knife-edge between the reality of which we have everyday knowledge, and the unreality which at all times surrounds it and on occasion threatens to engulf it.

Dreams are a very large subject indeed, and their interpretation is by no means uncontentious. We are entering a world of competing theories, and in the context of this book have not the space to elucidate them and even less the expertise to discriminate between them. Also, the very act of analysis in this area is fraught with difficulties. As Jung says, 'Becoming conscious is of course a sacrilege against nature, it is as though you had robbed the unconscious of something.' Robbed it, we must suppose, of the very attribute which gives it its uniqueness.

We propose to leave the whole area of the meaning of

dreams to others better qualified than ourselves, and to confine our observations and exercises to accessing and recalling, and the subsequent shaping of material. The approach will be an instinctive rather than an analytical one.

Jung also wrote, 'A dream is a theatre in which the dreamer is himself the scene, the player, the prompter, the author, the public and the critic.' So dreaming is a world which is entirely self-enclosed, in a sense self-created, and therefore of the utmost potential fascination to the individual. Yet, paradoxically, it is also a world over which the individual, by definition, can only exercise the most limited control. Later in this section we shall examine ways in which such intervention can be effective. But first of all it is necessary to concentrate upon what is given by the dream-process itself.

EXERCISE 48: A DREAM IMAGE

Often it is an image from a dream and the powerful feelings it evokes which we can recall rather than any narrative structure it possesses or the meaning we may assign to it. Concentrate upon an image that stays with you – maybe it is one which recurs in your dreams, or perhaps it was so powerful when experienced that it has never been forgotten. Flow-Write on it for two minutes and see what vivid details are thrown up.

EXERCISE 49: DREAM DIARY

Just as it is helpful to keep a journal of the thoughts, feelings and images that occur to you at the times when you are not concentrating upon writing, so it is helpful to keep a notepad by your bed to enter dreams as you come out of them. The mind can be trained to be more aware of dream-states and to develop the habit of recording them. Concentrate over a period of some weeks on making entries into a Dream Diary, then sit down with your jottings and select one to write in

full. As you focus upon it, more details will come to mind
and enable you to fill out the picture. This will leave you
with a permanent record of this particular dream-state or
provide you with material you could make into a poem
or story. Here is a diary jotting that John entered, followed
by the poem which he subsequently made from it:

> Lovely feeling, lovely dream. Erotic and happy. Walking in a
> garden. Enclosed by high walls. Greenhouses at one end. I feel
> impelled to visit them. All smashed up and in decay. But one
> seems special. Lots of foliage. Something glowing: a camellia.
> Wonderful in all this neglect. Can't tear my eyes from it. There's
> a little disc on a stick in the soil identifying it. On it is printed
> X's name. I can't see anything of her but feel sexually aroused.
> The whole day, the whole dream is transformed by this discovery.

> And now I am enclosed
> by high walls; enter this
> secret midwinter world's
> sempiternal stasis:
>
> underfoot sodden leaves,
> raw sticks, lie where they fell.
> I pass through greenhouses
> neglected, cold, the paint
> peeling, some of the panes
> shattered, pipes furred with rust.
>
> Then I see it: startling
> crimson camellia –
> its petals firm-folded,
> illumining the gloom.
> Parting the leaves I find
> that the bloom bears her name.

EXERCISE 50: DEVELOPING A DREAM

Really you can only develop a dream by having another
dream along the same lines as the first, and sometimes this

can occur, but you can't force it to happen. What you can do, though, is to give your creative imagination the opportunity to get to work on the ideas or images presented. When John again considered the dream he described in EXERCISE 49, he realized that the feeling of happiness he experienced only came at the end, and his poem reflected that. The predominant feeling was desolation, loss, and he decided to explore this further. So he concentrated on the feeling of being hemmed in; he Clustered the word 'enclosed':

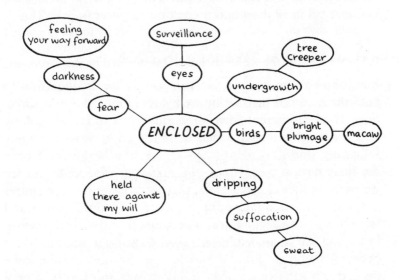

This seemed to lead in a quite different direction, and to seem 'right' in the same way that the garden, greenhouse and camellia seemed 'right'. The following piece came from the Cluster:

> I stood in the clearing: the tree-creepers dripped, the undergrowth rustled. I couldn't see the eyes looking at me, but I heard the cries of the birds, saw once a bright flash of plumage – was it a macaw? – felt the suffocating air (like the bathroom after, when you wipe away the sweat only to find another layer there).

As for the fear, it was like when you step out at night when there are no stars and you have to foot-feel your way forward, only there it was daylight, or what passes for daylight in the forest. I can't really express what it was like, except to say I was sure (surer than I've ever been anywhere else) that there was no place for me there.

So now John has two pieces of writing to set against each other – one ending in human contact of the most positive kind, and the other in alienation. They both hold a significance for him and stem from the same kind of dream. See if you can produce a second piece by this process.

EXERCISE 51: ACTIVE IMAGINATION

But John can go further. He can use Active Imagination to take the material thrown up by his dreaming in a new direction. The term comes from Jung and refers to image-making as a conscious process. It can be practised most immediately following upon a dream-state, where you lie awake letting the imagination work upon the material presented, and see where the process takes you. Alternatively (and this requires practice) you meditate upon a past dream until your mind has entered the feeling-area it occupied and is receptive to following up new leads. At this stage you are half-way between being in control and letting the unconscious take over. It is a kind of controlled day-dream and can be a very productive process.

John practised Flow-Writing in relation to his original dream and found himself in a very different kind of garden, a public rather than a private place, where the sexual element became threatening rather than fulfilling. Again the piece of prose is followed by the poem it grew into:

The garden is stifling, crowded, inturned. I am fighting for breath and space, cannot feel at ease here. People everywhere obscuring the flowers, which are neatly tended in beds and rows. The garden is attached to somewhere, a building, like one of those old mental hospitals with small windows, red-brick tall chimneys. I'm walking the paths, looking for a place to sit. Finally some men make room for me. They seem friendly, chatty, faintly conspiratorial. I could almost like them, but something holds me back. Then one starts to leer, another makes sexual innuendoes. I find myself surrounded, they're going to rape me. I yell, but no-one takes any notice. I wake myself up.

> I am in a garden
> formal, crowded, introvert.
> Men are moving around
>
> in ones, twos, small groups.
> The seats are spaced
> regularly, all full.
>
> Over the wall I see
> the chimneys, towers
> of an institution.
>
> I admire the tended
> flower-beds, all
> nodding heads
>
> in rows, like the men.
> I find a space,
> squeeze in between,
>
> start to converse:
> weather the one
> element left to chance.
>
> But soon their chat
> takes on cajoling
> tones. They turn, begin
>
> molesting me. They
> hold me hard. I scream
> and scream . . . no-one comes.

Now use Active Imagination to get inside one of your own dreams, and Flow-Write from within that state of mind.

Compare the results with those obtained by the Clustering you did in EXERCISE 50. Can you trace the progressive deepening of vision throughout this section?

EXERCISE 52: DREAM DIALOGUES

These represent a further development of the Active Imagination approach. You imagine yourself in the role of a person or object or idea in your dream and enter into conversation with them. This in turn has the capacity to spark off further insights, and provide new opportunities for writing. John imagined a conversation with one of his companions in the formal garden:

SELF:	What is this place?
OLD MAN:	Where we've always lived.
SELF:	What do people do here?
OLD MAN:	Obey the rules.
SELF:	How do we know what they are?
OLD MAN:	Oh, you follow what you have been taught by those older and wiser than yourself.
SELF:	Will you teach me how to behave?
OLD MAN:	Of course, I have a duty to instruct you.
SELF:	What if I say no, and leave?
OLD MAN:	You'll find you can't get away. There are far too many here for you to avoid being restrained. We are the moral majority.
SELF:	But that's nonsense. I've never taken that much notice of other people's views. I've always followed my own conscience.
OLD MAN:	What you want means nothing here. It's what's best for others that matters. How else could all of us survive in this restricted space?
SELF:	I'd rather die than submit to what you want.
OLD MAN:	Very likely you will. But we'll take our pleasures first.

Now choose some aspect of your dream to dialogue with. It could be a person, an object or a feeling.

EXERCISE 53: WRITING FROM PAINTINGS

Far more artists than writers have taken their inspiration from dreams, and perhaps that is not surprising as the intensely visual nature of dream-imagery lends itself more obviously to recreation in paint than in words. Those of us exploring through the latter medium, however, can avail ourselves of works by masters of art to put us in touch easily with the language of dreams. Postcards or illustrations from books allow us to familiarize ourselves with particular painters and find those who speak most sympathetically to us of our own experience of dreaming. Even within the oeuvre of an individual artist it may be only one or two paintings which strike a chord. Once found, these works can exercise a profound influence on the mind and on one's writing.

Some of the artists you might like to explore in search of inspiration are Chagall, Rousseau, Magritte, De Chirico, Ernst, Dali, Redon and Paul Nash. When you have found your painter, the one whose vision approximates most nearly to your landscapes of the mind, select a reproduction and study it for two or three minutes. This should not just be a matter of noting the details, it is more a matter of absorbing the atmosphere it creates. Now do a Cluster or Flow-Write on it. This will almost certainly give you further imaginative leads to follow up in prose or verse. The following example is from a Flow-Write based upon Chagall's painting *My Village*:

> And the within is without and the without is within. And all division is gone. And inside each within is a further within. And I am always climbing, struggling to get to the top, struggling to stay on the high mountainside – below me a dangerous drop and far below the blue blue sea. The sea cobalt, violet, and the little jetty that is forever my pier, the pier I travel back to.
>
> And here is the cow, my cow, the cows that made up my childhood, that are always in my head. Or is it that I am

the cow, that my head juts over everything, that my eye misses
nothing, that everything my eye sees is inside my cow head . . .

Anne Armley

EXERCISE 54: THE BIG DREAM

Writers *on* dreams and writers *of* dreams often make mention
of this very rare phenomenon, the dream which comes to
you surrounded by an aura of significance, as if the dream
is telling you to sit up (metaphorically) and take note
because it is to have a special solving or defining quality. It
is a dream that is likely to stay with you when you wake.
The message may be as much in the state of mind it induces
as in the symbolism it contains. There are a number of key
examples of 'The Big Dream' scattered through literature.
Edwin Muir was never guilty of forcing his unconscious to
deliver its secrets or jumping to conclusions about meanings.
Thus his poetry and prose constitute a treasure-house of
dream imagery. Here is a passage taken from his autobiography:

> I dreamed that I was standing at the bow of a boat; it was early
> morning, and the sky and the sea were milky-white. The ship
> went on with a rustling motion, and cut more deeply into the
> ever-deepening round of the horizon. A spire rose above the rim
> of the sea, and at once, as the ship rushed smoothly on, I could
> see the little streets, the prickly weeds growing out of the walls,
> the tangle dripping from the pier. The houses opened out, melted
> and ran together; in a moment I would be there; but then I saw
> that this was not the town I knew, and that the people walking
> about the streets were strangers. Then, the ship clean gone, I
> was wandering along the top of a high, craggy coast. Far beneath
> me the sea snarled in the caves, which like marine monsters
> gnashed at it and spat it out again; opposite across the boiling
> strait, so near that I felt I could touch it, was Rousay with its
> towering black mountain. I had never thought that this coast of
> Wyre was so wild and rocky, and even as this thought formed
> in my mind the isle grew tamer, grew quite flat, and I was

walking along a brown path level with the sea picking great, light, violet-hued, crown-shaped flowers which withered at once in my hands . . .

And this is not the end of this elaborate and densely patterned dream. If you have 'A Big Dream' that stays with you you could try writing it down, or as much of it as you can remember. Alternatively, any dream that you can recall in any detail would do for this exercise. Sit and think and feel your way into the dream before writing. Don't just write the outline of the dream, try to write under the influence of the feelings that accompanied it, so that your completed piece of writing is informed by them. Here is a dream that Myra had eight years ago which has stayed with her:

> I am driving a twelve-seater van and I feel a sense of satisfaction that I am able to manage such a large, solid vehicle with perfect control. I am also keyed up with expectation because I am on my way to a literary meeting which is also in some way a party. It is wonderful that I have been asked to it and I know it is going to be special, that it is a place where I belong, that the evening will be key in my life.
>
> To my dismay I find the van is stationary and people, strangers most of them, are piling into the van. They have a great many cases and they are all talking, telling me their names, which are confusing, and demanding lifts. Worse, they all ask for different destinations. I don't want these passengers. The places are miles away from this village where the party is. They will take me far out of my way and make me late, maybe even make me miss the event I am longing to get to. In any case I am also worried that the vehicle is overloaded and now I urge the people to get off but they say they need my help. I don't know how to refuse.
>
> We are parked in the middle of a beautiful village. I can see a spreading cedar and other evergreen trees, the high walls of great houses. And now I realize I am not sure which house or hall the party is in. I become more and more fraught. 'How shall I get there?' I scream as they argue and jabber their needs to me.

I want to throw them and their luggage out of the van but I am not powerful enough. At last I can't stand it any longer and struggle to a decision: to abandon the van and make a run for it. As I jump out, I wake up.

Drawing as a Stimulus

In this section we are going to ask you to take a different medium as a starting point and to try out a series of techniques which in the first stage don't require words at all. We believe this mode will offer a new area of possibilities. What we have in mind is drawing with coloured pens or, if you prefer, painting.

We are not suggesting you try to create a work of art or even to finish a picture unless you wish to. It doesn't matter if you haven't touched a paintbrush since you left school or if you are hopeless at drawing. The intention is simply that you represent incidents, situations, feelings and thoughts in pictorial form for your own use.

Shape, colour, size, position are very emotive and of course we often experience ideas and feelings as images. When we think about a person who arouses strong emotion in us such as love or jealousy we almost certainly visualize that person's face. When people say they are terrified of spiders they probably visualize the creature as they speak.

It is also very common to express states of mind and moods in words that suggest a picture. How often do we talk about being boxed in, seeing light at the end of a tunnel, walking on air, feeling small, big? It is not unusual for people to express a predicament or a state of mind by drawing it –

a figure wandering in a maze, a body trapped inside a metal pipe, and so on.

Artists reveal their inner worlds in their paintings. Van Gogh's claustrophobic corridors, the turbulent lines and colours in some of his skies, the joyousness of his apple trees in blossom immediately come to mind. Very different visions have been painted by Stanley Spencer and Howard Hodgkin.

Before you begin these exercises equip yourself with a packet of coloured felt tip pens or a box of watercolours or some tubes of acrylic paint. A4 typing paper will do if you are using felt tip pens but a book of cartridge drawing paper, A4 size or larger, would be better and will be necessary if you want to do paintings.

EXERCISE 55

In Part One: Getting in Touch with Feelings we asked you to write about a landscape in the past that was important to you. Now we'd like you to choose another outdoor place or an indoor place that has significance for you. It might be a childhood bedroom or garden, a place you visited once, a room or building or open space you escape to now for quiet, etc.

Draw it or paint it in any way you like. Don't feel any need to aim for realism. Be as fanciful, detailed, childish, decorative or expansive as you like. Include yourself and other people and/or animals if relevant in the picture and use shapes and colours to show how you are feeling. If your main memory of a room is its large table, for example, you might want to make the table very much larger than anything else in your picture. If you associate it with eating good meals, laughter and generous people you might want to reflect this by showing close-ups of the food, faces with soft curving lines and warm colours. If you associate the room with family rows, feel free to indicate this with sharp lines, heavy colours or in whatever way is meaningful to you.

Spend ten minutes – more if you want to – on your picture, then write about your chosen place with it in front of you. You may find the picture contains details that surprise you, that it moves you unexpectedly. Material may surface that you had forgotten or haven't formulated in words before. You may gain new insights about an event or situation you have been over many times.

EXERCISE 56

Choose a recent event in your life which you feel strongly about. It may be an occasion when you were very angry, worried, threatened, extremely happy, a moment of recognition, tranquillity, etc. If possible choose something you have not already written about. Now draw the incident, again using colour and shape in any way you like, to indicate your feelings. Be expansive when you depict yourself and anyone else who is involved. When you have finished write about the event using your picture as your starting point. Now repeat the exercise drawing on your past.

A few years ago, when working with an art therapist, Myra drew a picture of an incident that made her angry when she was eight years old. Her mother had taken her out to tea to a neighbour who promised her a sweet after tea. Tea came to an end but the sweets did not appear so the child reminded the neighbour about her promise. Afterwards her mother smacked her for asking for sweets. In her picture Myra drew herself lying on the carpet with her mother looming over her, still wearing her hat and coat. When she looked at her picture Myra was amazed by the violent red areas on the floor all round her. This was her anger and she was shaken that after many years she still felt so strongly about her unjust punishment. The representation of her anger gave it a reality, a validity that it didn't seem to have before. Soon after doing the drawing she wrote a poem called 'Boiled Sweets'. Expressing her feelings in words allowed the anger another channel and finally dealt with it. Here is part of the poem:

> Once a week she chose in the shop
> on the sea front, while the woman
> snipped from the ration book.
> A sweet was awarded after dinner
> on days she was good.
>
> By the hearth she held wool
> for her mother to wind, didn't mention
> the promise till the coats were fetched.
> Soon strawberry sweetness
> slipped down her throat.
>
> Outside mist chilled and she ran
> into the warmth of home. But mother,
> without taking off her hat,
> knocked her to the floor, tugged up
> her skirt, smacked her for asking.
>
> NOT FAIR, the words uncrunchable
> as metal bagatelle balls,
> cracked her feelings.
> Anger boiled out but seeped
> unseen into the carpet.

EXERCISE 57

Now focus on a time of change in your life. Let your picture show the change and its effect on you. If you prefer you can do two pictures, the first representing your life before the change, the second your life afterwards. Feel free to include diagrams, arrows and symbols, etc, for emphasis. When you have finished describe the change using your drawing for reference. (If you have written about this change in some way in an earlier exercise compare the two pieces of writing.)

Example

This is a picture of the time I confronted my mother head on at the top of her stairs. I had just been left by my first husband with two little boys. My mother had been widowed six months before. We went to stay with her in her house at the seaside. She put all three of us in one room. The boys were rustly and restless. In the morning I asked if she would put my oldest boy in the upstairs bedroom and she agreed. But didn't.

That evening I moved all his bedding, carried it upstairs and she was *there* suddenly at the stop of the stairs, immediately furious.

'What are you doing?' She tried a token push. But I didn't budge.

I said: 'We'll go back to London tonight unless you put him upstairs to sleep.' She grumbled but went down and left me to fix up his bed upstairs.

This first crucial battle lifted my spirits. I was able to face up to her after that, not always but when it was important.

Juliette Carter

EXERCISE 58

This is an opportunity to have some fun with fantasy. Visualize your ideal way of life – the surroundings you would like to live in, maybe with your perfect partner, how you would spend your time, your ambitions achieved, the travels you long to make, etc. Now 'realize' your fantasy by making as full a picture of it as you can. Be as extravagant as you like. Make yourself prominent in this vision. Finally write about your fantasy, mentioning your feelings and commenting on your new life.

EXERCISE 59

Now try using drawing to capture states and feelings which may be further removed from words. We have already explored dreams and the dream state, that area beyond everyday reality that we cannot control, which produces emotions and sensations which are haunting yet often difficult to pin down. Dreams usually occur as a series of images and, although words are significant in some dreams, in others they are of little importance or don't occur at all. This technique, therefore, is particularly suitable to use in connection with dreams.

Begin by drawing a recurrent dream. These often have very potent images: being pursued by a creature of which one has a phobic fear, walls collapsing, falling from a height, sitting in front of blank paper unable to write in an exam. (Poets are known to dream about doing readings and finding they can't decipher a single poem on the page in front of them! No doubt actors dream they have forgotten their parts!) If you have never had a recurrent dream, make one up. Write about the dream after you have drawn it.

Go on to draw a dream you've only experienced once which moved you strongly. Express it as fully as you can – in a series of pictures if this is appropriate. Fill the dream

out by making up details that fit in. If you can't remember
a dream, invent one by drawing a dream-like picture. Include
yourself in this fabrication and enjoy being inventive. Use
your picture(s) to write about the dream and your reactions
to it.

EXERCISE 60

Now we'd like you to use picture-making to take a direct
look at yourself – the sort of person you are, taking into
account your outer and inner life. Do two pictures in which
you loom large. Forget any idea of realistic portrayal or
formal art. In the first drawing we'd like you to bring out
what you see as negatives in your life. In the second picture
focus on what is positive in your life. You may want to
depict recurring or key incidents/feelings. Exaggerate as you
want to and try using pattern imaginatively or symbolically
to make your point. You can be impressionistic in your
approach or factually detailed. Enjoy finding ways of
expressing different sides of the person who you are. When
you have finished write about yourself in any way you like,
drawing on both pictures. You can do this as a composite or
move from one picture to the other. Ann Griswold has perceived this exercise as two visions with a connection between
them.

First Picture

I am running away in a turmoil – arms shaped like 'Cs' everywhere, reaching. My heart has left my body, exploded from my
chest. I am lost in the whirlwind of air, wind, screams, the harsh
caw of a crow. Black arrows pierce my scalp and the world is
ink-coloured.

Boundaries have blown away and I am scattered and many-
personed. My face is in another time, another place, patterned
in a scream, arms outstretched, reaching for balance. I am slipping in the wet treacherous grass underfoot. There are notes and
chords in the air, jumbled and atonal. Myself I am blinkered.

First Picture

Second Picture

Later when the winds calm down I open my eyes and smile shark-like, still frightened by the earlier nightmare. Above me the sky is quiet with the rising crescent moon. I might fly now; there's a bird on my head and a plane crosses the sky with dragonfly ease. Serenity is the grey cat beside me silvery as a teaspoon. He guards the mermaid hidden inside him and forms a bridge to the ocean, the mountains and a solid oak forest.

Second Picture

Myself, I am still many-faced: thoughtful, curious, sad with tears and a glass to hold them. My life is anchored to my house, Number 7, and my chorus of friends who line up and smile: 'Cheese please,' from the bottom of the picture. Their hands clasp over my tears and there is freedom in the bird-flight high over the hills, the forest. 'The Lord is my shepherd. I shall not want.'

EXERCISE 61

The next exercise invites you to move right away from the figurative. Choose a feeling you often experience or one that you experienced frequently in the past: fear, excitement, anger, determination, anxiety, sensuous enjoyment, disappointment, uncertainty, hope, envy, affection, etc. Write the feeling at the top of your paper and then try expressing it simply in shape, line and colour. Don't work out what might be appropriate or attempt to control what you are doing. Simply take colours that suggest themselves and let go. If you find yourself scribbling circles or spikes or downward curves, don't feel you must stop because the sheet looks a mess. Try out other shapes, images, colours as your hand guides you or as they suggest themselves.

Do a representation of a very different feeling you experience. Now choose one of the pictures and Flow-Write about it for a few minutes. Do the same with the other picture if you would like to.

Repeat the exercise with a feeling that you would like to experience but rarely or never do or with a feeling that you know you avoid.

Example

This is my anger. It's been jumping up and down, shouting to get out. Here it is spouting in a snorting black and red volcanic eruption. Its main column is hotter than boiling tar and, as it spreads out coughing ashes, it begins to solidify and reveal hooked claws. It will scorch, rip, obliterate anything in its way.

It is full of mouths that show thick teeth and red holes. It carries thunderbolts and black crosses that will strike out. When it has consumed all the objects of its rage it will wipe out all the things I want to keep. It will appropriate the air. It will consume me. What can I do with this anger without destroying myself?

Stephen Nelson

EXERCISE 62

We now invite you to represent your reactions to a particular event, day in your life, person you have just met, an ambition or place you have visited as an abstract. Proceed as you did in the previous exercise and again Flow-Write with the drawing or painting in front of you.

EXERCISE 63

Finally, we'd like to suggest you try doing a mandala, which is a drawing inside a circle. A circle, often with an image or a pattern inside it, has been a symbol in religion and religious art for a very long time. More recently Jung saw it as a symbol of the wholeness of the self. Creating drawings or patterns inside a circle is often used now in art therapy. This way of expressing a state of mind or reaction can be very satisfying and healing.

Draw a circle, now close your eyes and concentrate on a feeling, event, conversation, person or your present mood for a minute or two. When you feel ready use your felt-tipped pens to make a picture within the circle using any mixture of pattern and figurative drawing that suggests itself. Then Flow-Write about your mandala or use it as the basis of an Image Exploration or an Internal Dialogue between different parts of yourself. If you would like to find out more about mandalas and explore this technique in detail read *Creating Mandalas* by Suzanne F. Fincher.

PART THREE

Inner and Outer

The Body

We are housed in our bodies, experience the world through them and they therefore play a crucial part in what we feel and think. Furthermore, outward appearance, voice, our mannerisms, the way we hold ourselves are all features of our personalities. If we are exploring ourselves in writing we cannot ignore our bodies. In this section we offer some introductory exercises which invite you to look at your relationship with your body.

EXERCISE 64

We perceive the world through our five senses – sight, hearing, touch, smell and taste. It could be argued that touch is the most basic as it relates to every part of our bodies. It is a sense that is sometimes taken for granted.

a) Spend a few minutes making a list of touch sensations you enjoy and another of touch sensations you dislike. Now Flow-Write about touch for a few minutes and/or choose a touch sensation from one of your lists and Flow-Write about this.

b) Explore your sense of smell using the Clustering technique to give you material for a piece of writing.

c) In the voice of your eyes, ears or mouth write a monologue about what you like and hate experiencing.

Example of Flow-Writing about Touch

Your touch was the warm sand on summer beaches, safe hand to hold on a crowded platform, ice cold hands lifting me out of a snow drift, warm breath on my cheek, cheek touching my lips to say goodbye, skin warm to my touch as you lay stiller than I'd ever seen you. I touched your arm, expecting coolness – surely no one could lie so still and still be alive. I expected nurses to come and tell me: 'Don't touch.' But no one came. I couldn't touch you again – there was no way to know what you needed – you seemed in a world beyond touch – might my touch cause you pain? or be the most wished for thing – how to know? I wanted so much to touch you again but went away.

Liz Houghton

EXERCISE 65

We'd like next to concentrate on the different parts of the body.

a) Choose either your hands or your feet and look carefully at your hands or bare feet. Now spend a few minutes writing a description of your hands/feet and bring in your feelings about them.

b) Choose one aspect of your hands/feet that you would like to focus on. It might be something you do with them regularly: e.g. cooking, dancing, playing the violin, cross country running, etc., or it might be a particular incident or situation in which you were aware of them. With this aspect in mind write about your hands/feet using Flow-Writing or Clustering.

Example

These are my hands and I used them to steal. The first time I stole Julie's chocolate from the fridge. It was three in the morning and I was desperate to fill my emptiness. Cake followed biscuits,

sweets followed cake. The cake was for a family in size but it
went in seconds. And then there was nothing of mine left to
swallow, and my empty bits had grown and grown. So these
hands stole Julie's chocolate from the fridge. It was Tesco's own
brand cake-covering chocolate.

I added remorse to the emptiness, and these hands went to
Tesco's and replaced the chocolate from the fridge. But the emptiness grew.

In Tesco's these hands seized a magazine. An article called 'Eat
as Much as You Like' pleaded with my hands to be taken from
the shelf. These hands held the magazine as I walked out of the
shop without thinking to pay. But the hands that held the magazine didn't fill the emptiness.

These hands are guilty hands, hands that have done wrong,
and they regret. They can't fill the emptiness. These hands are
tied.

Lesley Davies

Alison Chisholm also produced a piece of writing about
hands using the Clustering technique and she used the
material to write a poem which she tightened later on. Here
it is:

Contact

Ritual done, sterile as Pilate
the team of surgeons gathers,
cuts, excises, cleanses.

Bloodied gloves are binned.
Your hands, my father, are the lifeline
for liquids dripping in,
for pulsebeats measured out.

Practical hands; your gestures make
a mime of actions showing how they stripped
the pins that stitched your chest.
And I remember watching
your hands at plane and chisel,
your fingers threading my shoelaces.

> And suddenly I do not know
> how to hold your hand. A nurse
> sits with me, her arm across my shoulders,
> twines my fingers around yours
> to catch their last warm moments.
>
> Before I leave, pick up the life you gave me,
> I wash my hands.

c) Now choose any two other parts of your body to write about: hair, eyes, throat, teeth, shoulders, stomach, ears, breasts, penis, etc. Use Flow-Writing to write about one, Clustering to write about the other.

EXERCISE 66

List the parts of your body which cause you problems and note down the problem beside each body part, eg stomach because it's easily upset; legs because they are short. Now list the parts of your body which are assets to you, also with notes, eg eyes because I love painting, hair because its chestnut colour makes me attractive. Now write a dialogue which is an argument between a part of the body which is an asset to you and a part which causes problems in which each states its case and criticizes the other.

Example

BACK: I have to support the rest of the body but now that I'm in pain I get no support at all.

FACE: Oh stop complaining! She's taken you to three different osteopaths but do you respond – not you! You just go on moaning and keeping the rest of us awake all night. You're spoiling my looks.

BACK: Your looks aren't anything very wonderful with all those lines. In fact you never were much of a beauty.

FACE: I never said I was. But I'm warm and soft and people love me. However, if I don't get some rest I'll look like an old witch and it will be your fault.

BACK: That's unkind, spiteful.

FACE: What are you doing all hunched on the settee?

BACK: I'm giving up. Everyone and everything's against me. I'll never get better.

FACE: Oh come on. You're not ready for the rubbish heap yet. You can still carry the legs. I'm sorry I snapped at you.

Maria Knowles

EXERCISE 67

Make a list of bodily experiences you enjoy. They might include some of the following: walking, swimming, and other forms of exercise, sport, cuddling, sex, eating, relaxing in a bath, etc. Write a sentence about one activity and its effect on you. Then Flow-Write about it.

EXERCISE 68

Language, spoken, written or signed, is the formal means by which we communicate, but our bodies play an important part in what we communicate. The tone in which we speak, the pitch of voice, how easily we talk, the amount we laugh, frown, smile and show other facial expressions, our gestures, postures and all kinds of individual mannerisms – coughs, clearing the throat, key phrases, small hand movements, flicking one's hair, etc, etc, convey messages directly to other people. They also affect the meaning of the words we speak. Unless you already feel very familiar with these details of your body's behaviour we suggest you observe yourself in different situations for a day or two before you try the following:

a) Flow-Write about your voice or one of your mannerisms.

b) Write a paragraph describing how you sit, talk, gesture when you are with a person or people with whom you feel at ease.

c) Now write a paragraph about your body's behaviour in a situation with another person or people you find difficult.

EXERCISE 69

As our bodies grow, mature and age our needs, attitudes, feelings and behaviour change. In Jaques' famous 'seven ages' speech in *As You Like It*, Shakespeare identifies the different stages we pass through in life with telling details about the body.

a) Describe your appearance in as much detail as you can at a particular age between three and eleven. If at all possible use a photograph to help you.
b) Look in a mirror and describe yourself now.
c) Using Drawing as a Stimulus, Dialogue or another technique write about the differences and similarities you see between your appearance now and at some other stage in your past.

EXERCISE 70

Our bodies play a central part in some of our most powerful experiences. Write about one of the following using Narrative, Clustering, Flow-Writing or Dramatization: puberty, first or other sexual experience, pregnancy, childbirth, fathering a child, ageing, a serious illness or accident, the prospect of death.

Example

He lay on top of me, banging his pelvis against mine. The old divan bed creaked under the desperation of his attempt. I lay quiet, waiting for the great happening; my stomach felt queasy with his heavier body lunging at mine.

'Put your legs apart!' His voice was disgusted. A great shame crept over me; I didn't even know the positions for intercourse. My feet moved until my legs made a narrow V on the rumpled khaki blankets.

'Up!' he commanded and I turned my face to the pillow and raised my ankles six inches up from the bed. Now he was kneeling on the tattered linoleum beside the bed pulling at my knees.

I couldn't participate after that; it was too deep a humiliation that I had to be arranged correctly for love. What else had I missed? He grabbed at my breasts and kneaded them vigorously like bread rolls, groaned, sweated stomach to stomach, entered with a lot of thrusting and pounding. I lay inert and cold as a cucumber sandwich, bruised and battered and surprised. What was all the fuss about? [...]

'Happy?' he asked, stroking the hair at the back of my neck, attempting to be tender.

I didn't know how to answer; the soreness between my legs proved I was a woman. I'd grown up and my new sophistication pleased me [...] The theory was grand, but in practice it seemed such a let-down. It hurt, lying there letting it all happen. Should I pretend different?

Ann Stevens

EXERCISE 71

Here are some other body topics: energy, exhaustion, tension, sleep/insomnia, blood, weight, pain, clothes. Choose one and write about it in relation to yourself using the Clustering technique.

EXERCISE 72

Whatever our feelings they are reflected in our bodies. Anxiety makes the neck and shoulders tense. It may make the head ache. Breath is shallow, fast and uneven if we panic, etc. There is a growing understanding in the medical world of the link between body and mind. Note down two feelings, one positive, one negative that you often feel: eg anxiety, guilt, anger, excitement, amusement, hope, etc. Now write a few sentences describing how each of these affects your body. Try this exercise again after observing in detail how your body reacts to the feelings.

EXERCISE 73

We end with two exercises which use the body as a starting point. They are inspired by John Lee's *Writing from the Body* which we recommend especially if you would like to go further into your relationship with your body. First of all do *one* of the following activities (without over-straining in any way). Notice how your body behaves and how you feel:

a) Sit comfortably, close your eyes and concentrate on your breathing, letting it get slower and deeper. After a couple of minutes or so take a deep breath, allowing your chest to expand and after three seconds let go, allowing all tension to flow out of you. Leaving short intervals take two more deep breaths. Then return to your usual breathing and when you are ready open your eyes.

b) Find some lively music to listen to on the radio or a CD and dance/move round the room in any way you like to the music for a few minutes or else enjoy yourself singing aloud.

c) Do some energetic cleaning in the house or strenuous work in the garden for a while or run until you are out of breath.

d) Go swimming, take part in a sport you enjoy, or go for a brisk walk.

As soon as you can after completing the activity, describe it, concentrating on your sensations and feelings, then move into Flow-Writing. Repeat this exercise with a different activity. Here are two extracts from pieces of writing done at the same workshop after concentrating on breathing:

> When I stop breathing I shall stop living. Plants breathe, animals breathe, for all we know stones may breathe, may be alive. I remember reading a story about a tomato that shed tears when a knife sliced through it.
>
> When I became conscious of my breathing it slowed down. We all need to slow down sometimes. I shall never forget the 14th of April, sitting opposite my mother's bed, with nothing to do but watch her breathing, and registering the moment when she did not breathe any longer.
>
> *Joy Winterbottom*

> I can't get where I want to. It's too hard. I lug this heavy body around when I want to leave the ground and fly. My own person comes between me and what I want to be, panting, anxious, frightened, straining, stuck in my own mud. The spirit can't free itself and fly.
>
> So whither now, what advice do I give myself? Breathe slow, so slow I sink to a greater calm, slow as the bark growing round the trees, slow as the morning before the day begins.
>
> *Elke Dutton*

EXERCISE 74

This is an Image Exploration which uses the body. (It is a good idea to ask someone to give you the instructions for the actions in the first part. If that is not practical, go over the stages until you can remember them.) Stand up or lie down and close your eyes. Focus for a few moments on the images and sensations behind your eyes. Keeping your eyes closed, stretch out your arms and legs and imagine you can reach far into the world. Notice land, sea and sky features. Now, imagine your fingers finding and grasping something, perhaps something you want. Bring your cupped hands towards your stomach. Visualize what you are holding. When you are ready open your eyes, go to your notebook and Flow-Write about this experience.

Relationships, Families and Other Groups

Relationships

Our relationships with individuals play a crucial role in our lives, in particular the relationships we have with our parents, siblings, partners, lovers, children, close friends and sometimes work partners or associates. In Part Two: Tapping Into Memory we asked you to look at people who mattered to you in your early life and you are likely to have touched on relationships elsewhere. We begin this section by suggesting techniques for investigating your relationships more closely.

EXERCISE 75

Make a list of all the people who have had a key role in your life. Choose one who is central to you now. Write a secret letter to him/her about your relationship, what is happening in it, what is working, not working, your overall feelings about it.

EXERCISE 76

Go back to your list and choose someone who was important to you in the past. Write about your relationship with this person, encapsulating its main features, its effect on you and what it means to you, using Clustering, Flow-Writing, Modelling, Narration or Drawing as a Stimulus or a combination of techniques. Repeat this exercise with any other people on the list you want to write about. Here is part of a spontaneous piece of writing by Nina Lazarus about the close bond between herself and her grandfather:

> The smell of the timbers and the whirring of the bandsaw was enough to draw me like a magnet to his bench. He was always glad to see me and would give me a cuddle. 'You can count out the screws for me and give the glue a few stirs.' They were such simple tasks but he managed to make me feel important.
>
> He never found it strange that an eleven-year-old girl preferred to spend most of her spare time in a workshop rather than going out with her friends. 'All knowledge is good,' he said as he taught me all the names of the woods and the tools: bradall, spokeshave, brace and bit.
>
> When I wasn't busy being his 'little apprentice' I would sit on an upturned box swinging my legs, listening to stories of his fleeing Russia in the clothes he stood up in. As well as his pet subject, his craft, granddad could hold an interesting conversation on almost anything. He loved books and was extremely well-read.
>
> The times I spent with him in the workshop were the happiest days of my life. We shared our secrets and he was intensely loyal – never betrayed a confidence. He not only enriched my childhood he provided the most precious thing of all – unconditional love.

Veronica Rospogliosi wrote about the triangle of herself, her father and her grandmother:

> My poor grandmother was so ridiculed and resented – the early bond I'd forged with her never forgiven. My widowed father blamed her for everything – that we'd not been taken to India, that he needed her help, that my mother had died. I was born into this anger. He didn't see me for two and a half years.
>
> I was always seen as 'on granny's side'. Not able to collude

in ridiculing her I was often rubbed raw. Over the years the radiance of my early childhood was scratched and splintered. She's still being demonized. I know she wasn't the jolliest person though that side of her has been over-denied. She and I had some good giggles. I always felt angry at my father's injustice and it was a threat and a serious upset to be the child of someone so mean-minded.

When I was about fifteen I turned on him: 'Why do you *always* run Granny down? She does so much for us – like seeing to our clothes and paying for them – you should be GRATEFUL to her.' I left the room. A few minutes later he came heavily upstairs and stood in my bedroom doorway breathing hard.

'You don't know what you're talking about.' He spoke jerkily, his breathing pained and excited. 'Grateful – I'll tell you this. She *undermined* our marriage.' His agitation was high but held in as though reining back from smashing his weight about, getting hold of me in hate/love/anger – from tearing me asunder. He didn't use many words. I nodded, speechless, waiting for him to go away.

EXERCISE 77

Now take an overall look at the relationships in your life. Do they seem to follow similar patterns? Do you have particular expectations from relationships? Which of your relationships are stressful, which enriching? Do you feel the need of intimacy with a lot of people or only a few? Do you enjoy spending periods of time on your own? Do you find it easy/difficult to make relationships? Do you have any feelings about this? Flow-Write about one or more of the above questions.

Groups

We are also shaped by the roles we play in the groups of people we belong to during our lives. Of these groups the unit (or different units) in which a child grows up has a lasting influence. What might outwardly appear a balanced home life: two parents who remain married, have no money worries, are solicitous for their children, spend time with them, make sure they have a good education and holidays, is never the kind of bland, trouble free group that a television commercial suggests.

There may be very little communication between the members of the family. One parent may dominate the whole family. The children may be over-protected so that they find it hard to cope with the real world. They may be subjected to constant criticism for not achieving enough. One child may always be favoured and the other, or one of the others, turned into a scapegoat. Poet Isobel Thrilling was put into this role as a child (*see* extracts from 'Mother' in Part Six: Loss). It may be difficult in adult life to come to terms with such problems.

If partners split up and their child or children have to rely on one parent or settle into a different family pattern, if a parent dies, if a child grows up or spends part of his/her childhood in an orphanage, if children are seriously neglected or physically abused, then clearly there will be deep and sometimes dramatic effects. Major changes in a family's circumstances such as loss of financial stability or the move to another country as refugees also have a profound influence. In *Twopence to Cross the Mersey* Helen Forrester describes graphically the shock of moving to a poor area in Liverpool in the 1930s when her unpractical middle-class father lost his job and her mother was quite unable to cope emotionally. The 12-year-old Helen, who had lived a sheltered life in a household with a maid, suddenly found her role was to take charge of the youngest children.

If a grandparent or other relative lives with or so near to the family that he or she is part of the family group, or if a grandparent, aunt, etc. becomes the primary carer of a child or children, this will also be important. Sometimes the family relationship is so warm, the bond between the members so strong, that it is difficult for the child or children to find another group in later life that in any way measures up to the first one.

EXERCISE 78

Do a drawing or diagram of the family or main group in which you spent your childhood up to the age of twelve. Indicate by colour, shape and size your role in this group and the roles of its other members. With your drawing in front of you write a sentence about your position in this set up. Now Flow-Write about your role. Alternatively, write a Secret Letter to the other members or one of the other members of the group telling them how you feel about the role you had in it and the effect of this on your later life. Here is Clive Eastwood's perception of his role in the family he grew up in:

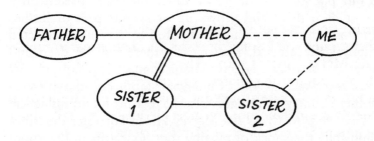

When I was about eleven I began to feel that I somehow didn't fit in with the rest, that the others all faced me side on.

It was a bit like being on the outside of a circle of school friends, except I don't remember making much effort to jump up, to try to see what was in the circle, what they found so interesting. I was the eldest. In the drawing it is as though the triangle of my mother and two sisters is between me and my father. At this age we didn't have much direct communication with him anyway – my mother was the intermediary. It was as if I wanted to be separate because I couldn't be a part – but of course I was still too young, too dependent. There was never any overt exclusion. I just seemed not to feel the sort of things they felt, seemed not to feel them the same way. I wasn't unhappy but I don't remember being happy either.

EXERCISE 79

Turn your attention to the family or group you were living in during your teenage years. The individuals may be the ones who were in your childhood group but with the changes of puberty it is likely your perception of the group changed and maybe your role in it. Repeat the drawing/diagram part of EXERCISE 78, applying it to yourself at an age between thirteen and eighteen. With the diagram in front of you write a dramatic scene or relate from your point of view an incident or recurring situation which shows how this group operated.

EXERCISE 80

During your formative years there are likely to have been other groups you belonged to which had an important influence. Make a list of them. They might include a class at school, groups of children you played with, clubs, etc. Choose one of these groups and make up a dialogue between yourself and one or more members in which you talk about the group. Show the part it played in your life.

Example: The Boys in B Dorm at Prep School

ME: There were about a dozen of us. We were nine years old.

MACLEAN: I was only eight. Robinson was still wetting the bed.

BRADY: That was you, Maclean. You were always in the bed-wetters' club.

MACLEAN: Well, you had impetigo!

ME: We were hungry all the time and it was freezing. Those blankets were so thin you could *see* through them.

MACLEAN: I didn't wet the bed. I *can't* have.

ME: I was told to keep an eye on you in case you ran away.

BRADY: He got as far as St Albans once.

MACLEAN: Why can't I remember?

BRADY: I remember being beaten and caned – and I remember none of us ever sneaking on the others. Yes, and I remember that sawn-off golf club the Headmaster used to use. The bastard used to beat us like rugs. Do you remember matron?

ME: Yes. I remember going to her when I couldn't sleep – very late. She used to give me an aspirin – and a cuddle. I used to go back night after night.

John Sandridge

EXERCISE 81

Adult life, especially today, is lived in many different patterns. Although many stay with one partner and bring up one family, increasing numbers of people change the partner they first of all settle down with. Some have more than one family, even keep close contact with more than one family. Many people leave behind one or more relationship and settle into bringing up children on their own or living by themselves. Some prefer the freedom of being independent, enjoy pleasing themselves and meeting who they want to, when they want. Others in this situation feel isolated and at times depressed but can find no better alternative.

Mobility has increased greatly during this century and many people move far from the locality they were born in. Although there are still strong extended family groups, adult siblings often have less contact with each other and less with their parents than in previous generations. Many children grow up seeing less of their grandparents, aunts, uncles and cousins than in previous generations. In this world of smaller units, individuals find different ways of operating as groups/ networks. Close friends talk regularly on the phone. Elderly couples who live in an area where they have few or no friends, are phoned frequently, even daily, by their children and grandchildren. A group of friends becomes a close unit because they share the same orientation. Six or seven women, who no longer have a partner, meet regularly to share their problems. Workmates go to the pub together on a Friday evening. Small groups of writers meet to look at their work in close detail. Others with an interest or need in common form intimate units in which to share some aspect of their lives.

There are, of course, more formal set ups: people who work together, ethnic groups, pressure groups, tenant groups, support groups for those who are overweight, suffer from the same illness, have a common problem, also clubs for people with the same interest and so on.

Do a drawing/diagram and use colour/size/shape to show the groups you belong to now and their relative importance to you. With the drawing in front of you, describe the part groups play in your life and then move into Flow-Writing.

Example

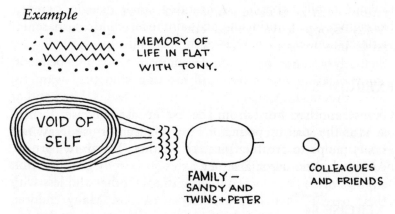

Tony, my partner for ten years, left me two months ago for a younger man. Since he went I have been no-one, living in a void. I work badly, sleep badly, get by because I have been a journalist long enough to produce stuff automatically but my writing hasn't a spark of life. I ought to sell the flat and move because the ghost of the happiness I once had is all round me, stinging me. God knows why but Sandy has forgiven me for leaving her and living with Tony. Going round to her house – what was *our* house – quite often, the sense of the twins there even though they're now away at college, the kindness of Sandy and Peter, the partner she has – a quiet man who's partly paralysed but who never moans about his problems – being allowed to be part of the family I took myself away from – is the only thing that's kept me alive. Friends at work, in the pub, the squash club, other couples apart from Chris and Tom – I can't face. The essential I gone – what is left is a dummy except for the odd half hour when I manage to forget that I am an entity at all.

Rupert Hill

Repeat the exercise in relation to an earlier stage in your adult life.

EXERCISE 82

Use the Clustering technique to write about one of the following: family, couple, separation, single, single parent, belonging, team, intimacy, acquaintance, children, parents victimization, equality, relationship, friendship.

EXERCISE 83

Choose another word from the list in last exercise. Either use it as the starting point for Flow-Writing or use Drawing as a Stimulus to create a piece of writing. The drawing can be representational or abstract.

EXERCISE 84

Write a letter to yourself from a real or imaginary insightful friend commenting on the way your life has changed over the years in terms of the groups of people you are involved with and offering helpful suggestions about changes you might want to make in the future. This is how Clive Eastwood tackled this exercise.

Dear Clive,
It's good to hear the fourth age is going well. If you make it to Shakespeare's seven then there should still be exciting times ahead. I feel that the three big dividing lines so far in your life were:

a) leaving home for college
b) getting married
c) breaking up the marriage.

But have you noticed how few contacts from each of these phases survived into the next one? Each time you change your life all the people you have mixed with disappear. Apart from the kids you don't really mix with anyone you socialized with before the divorce. Understandable in a way but were they all joint friends or her friends? Didn't you have any of your own who might have stayed loyal to you? A word of advice – don't close down. As time goes on people become more important, it gets harder to break new ground.
Best wishes,
Tom

Inner Traits and Outside Influences

In looking inwards it is easy for people to adopt a negative stance, dwelling upon their feelings of inadequacy and the mistakes that they have inevitably made in their lives, while neglecting to give due weight to the qualities and the achievements. Far more people go into therapy because they have problems which urgently require addressing than those who wish to engage in self-development for its own sake. In this section we will be suggesting exercises which will help to promote a balanced view of the self.

EXERCISE 85: AFFIRMATIONS AND NEGATIONS

This exercise resembles EXERCISE 18 in which the likes and dislikes of Edwin Morgan's poem range across the whole of personal experience; here they are inward-turned. Affirmations and Negations are the ways in which the mind is continually telling us about our own performance. It is the balance that we achieve between the two which largely determines whether our approach to future experience will be successful or not. Write a series of pairs of sentences about yourself commencing 'I am . . .' and 'I am not . . .' Give yourself five minutes of writing as spontaneously as possible in this vein, and then examine what has emerged, selecting the most interesting, or those which grouped together will form the most coherent whole, to make a short piece, as in the following:

Example One

Paradoxes

I am sociable.
I am not at ease in large groups of people.

I am a lover of solitude and silence.
I am not reserved.

I am full of colour.
I am not bright today but dulled with anxiety.

I am a person who wears feelings like a scarf patterned with
   flowers.
I am not able to show all my harsh red anger.

R Jenkinson

Example Two

My Life as a Butterfly

I am short-lived: from chrysalis to creature in a matter of minutes.

I am not able to settle easily, I alight and am away almost before
   anyone notices.

I am of the earth, and yet require air for flight.

I am not easily caught and cupped in the hand.

I am handsome, though that is not something which concerns
   me.

I am not able to protect my wings from dismembering.

I am conscious that once dead you can be kept in a box for a
   long time.

I am not going to waste a second of precious purposefulness.

Andrew Newton

This second piece suggests a personality-trait – that of

optimism in the face of adversity. It could be one of the writer's most significant characteristics.

EXERCISE 86: CHECK-LIST OF TRAITS

One of the simplest and most obvious methods of identifying traits is the check-list. Here are some of those aspects of the self most easily identified, alongside their opposites:

Secretive/Open	Humorous/Solemn
Spontaneous/Guarded	Conformist/Rebellious
Mean/Generous	Impulsive/Wary
Lazy/Hardworking	Materialistic/Spiritual
Talkative/Reserved	Stolid/Adventurous
Streetwise/Naïve	Serious/Light-hearted
Caring/Offhand	Moody/Equable
Shy/Outgoing	Enthusiastic/Placid
Brave/Timid	Gullible/Sceptical
Aggressive/Meek	Panicky/Unflappable

You could add some pairs of your own. Choose from the list those that seem most applicable (don't avoid those that appear challenging, as they may reveal more about you than the others), and cross out those alternatives which do not, in your view, describe yourself. You will be left with a rough-and-ready self-portrait. If you now read through the list that you have chosen perhaps a kind of pattern will begin to emerge. In making your crossings-out you may well have found it difficult in some (maybe most) instances to choose between the alternatives. It is obvious that we are not wholly one thing or another but occupy a position on the spectrum at some point between the two opposites. You may also have cause to reflect that we may each of us display elements of even the most unlikely qualities at one time or another.

Example

Two Sides of My Coin

Timid and tough,
strong and weak,
raging or calm,
wild or meek,
dangerous, careful,
sane or crazed,
it all depends on which surface is raised.

Being ever so humble,
flipping my lid,
behaviour outrageous,
doing as bid –
these pole oppositions,
which one of them's me?
Take up the coin
and flip it to see.

Ann Farry

EXERCISE 87: PORTRAIT OF A TRAIT

Now is the time to examine in detail some of the traits you
have identified. Choose one of them to Cluster. Make sure
that you concentrate upon the quality as it applies to yourself
and not in relation to another person or an abstraction. Turn
your Cluster into a piece of continuous writing. Then adopt
the same process with a number of other traits individually.
Here, by way of illustration, are, first of all, a piece written
as a result of Clustering the trait 'Spiritual', and secondly, a
piece which could have come from Clustering the word
'Lazy' but is in fact a piece written by a Chinese man in 811
AD, translated by Arthur Waley!

Example One

Spiritual

To me life is nothing without its spiritual dimension. From early adolescence I wanted to know the meaning of everything. I couldn't believe the answers orthodox religion offered, I couldn't see anything in religion except rules. I turned to Wordsworth – his poetry and pantheism – the sense of god in everything, the essential unity of life. I could connect with that. Nature, colour, paintings, and above all words and poetry are for me the ways to the inner world, the inner self whom I need to turn to in order to feel fully alive. And when I am away from noise, in its stillness, I wonder at the intricate patterns in the world, at the power of what human beings create, the horror of what we destroy, at our capacity to survive.

R Jenkinson

Example Two

Lazy Man's Song

I could have a job, but I am too lazy to choose it.
I have got land, but am too lazy to farm it.
My house leaks; I am too lazy to mend it.
My clothes are torn; I am too lazy to darn them.
I have got wine, but I am too lazy to drink:
So it's just the same as if my cup were empty.
I have got a lute, but am too lazy to play:
So it's just the same as if I had no strings.
My family tells me there is no more steamed rice;
I want to cook, but am too lazy to grind.
My friends and relatives write me long letters;
I should like to read them but they're such a bother to open.
I have always been told that Hsi Shu-yeh
Passed his whole life in absolute idleness.
But he played his lute and sometimes worked at his forge;
So even he was not as lazy as I.

Of course, our lives are not just made up of innate qualities. Many of our traits are learned or unconsciously absorbed from our surroundings. The rest of this section will be concerned with identifying and writing about what we term 'Outside Influences'.

We are each of us born into a country with a native language and culture. Within that country and culture we are born into a class or caste or distinctive social grouping. The economic circumstances of our family (or in the case of orphans the very lack of a family) will have a profound effect on our upbringing and educational opportunities. Our racial background, colour and gender will all condition our life-chances. The religion of our parents may to a greater or lesser degree prove a liberating or constricting force. Maybe at some stage of our lives we have left the country of our birth, its culture and its language behind. Perhaps we have entered a different society with different attitudes to racial background, colour and gender. Maybe our economic circumstances have changed and we have moved up or down the social ladder. These are just a few of the factors to be taken into account in attempting a more objective account of the outward circumstances of our lives to set beside the subjective approach to which this book is otherwise dedicated.

Although they are not in any sense distanced accounts, it is interesting to examine some of the writings in the Themes and Examples part of the book for traces of these factors. We suggest you turn to the pieces by Maya Angelou, Susan Wicks, Keith Waterhouse, Alfred Williams and Eva Hoffman. Read together they provide a vivid patchwork of life experiences in which outer influences have played a significant role.

EXERCISE 88: EVALUATING YOUR INFLUENCES

In this exercise you will attempt to assess the influences upon yourself. First you will need to list the factors which have played and continue to play a part in moulding the person you are. Then try to indicate what effects they have had upon you. Any changes in the influence of individual factors should also be noted. Here is Jane Birkett's attempt:

FACTORS	EFFECTS	CHANGES
Country	Wales - encouraged to be Patriotic	went to London after marriage - lost sense of national identity
Culture	Close Community in Valley - you either conformed or were an outsider	enjoyed diversity in City
Race	Part - British, part - West Indian	was able to Choose to mix or not - felt pull of both
Colour	Half-Caste leading to playground taunts, discrimination in Job-interviews	felt much less prejudice post-School
Class	Working-Class-father a Coal-miner, mother a Cleaner	moving up - became a Secretary, husband a shop Steward
Gender	Female - expectations of domestic role	adopted ideals of career and equality
Religion	Non-conformist Chapel-regular enforced attendance	rejected organized religion when first moved, now inclining towards Baptist.

Now look at the table that you have filled in. Which of the factors do you consider has had the strongest effect upon you? Write further notes about it. Which of the factors has undergone the most change? Write further notes about that one too.

Now attempt to write an account in objective terms of the outward influences upon your life. Use the table you have compiled, giving due emphasis to those you have identified as the most significant factors and those which have been subjected to the most change. Allow yourself 500 words or more for this purpose. Here is the opening passage of Jane Birkett's attempt:

> The Welsh are a very independent people. And those who live in the Valleys are the proudest of them all. They have a working-class culture that is distinctive. And it is closely linked to the mines. The hard graft of working down the pit has conditioned the way things are. As a girl, from a very early age I learned that I had been born into a man's world. You had to be tough, families must support each other often through hard times, and you did your bit by playing second fiddle to father and brother, who swore, drank, sang their hearts out, and generally laid down the ground rules. You conformed or you were pummelled into submission. I grew up to see my role as that of a wife-and-mother solely . . .

EXERCISE 89: ANOTHER INFLUENCE

These influences are so important that we want to give you another opportunity to write about them. In the Tapping into Memory section we invited you to Flow-Write using an object or a photograph or a place or an incident as a stimulus. Choose one of these which is specifically related to an outside influence. Or attempt a drawing, as suggested in the Drawing as a Stimulus section, to start you off. Then work on your piece until you are satisfied that it thoroughly explores the theme. Here is an example of a poem by Sue Hubbard which vividly recreates the realization of her racial origins:

Inheritance

Childhood Sundays: the dread
and the polished patina of oak
with crimson claret, the snowy
linen in initialled silver rings
and hexagrams of cutlery on
table mats of hunting scenes –
pink coats and fox-hounds braying
for the kill and my father skilfully
carving the strained lacunae
thin as slices of rare beef.
Days when grandma came, the air
was sharp as English mustard
– she wouldn't eat the meat,
instead brought pots of pickled
cucumber, chopped liver, balls
of gefilte fish wrapped in waxy paper-bags
which made my mother sigh.
'It's not kosher' grandma said
when I asked why? unlocking
clouded memories, three generations'
climb from East End tenement
to this wooded Surrey hill.
This was a house of tea cups,
of cupboards layered with shelves
of my father's crisp starched shirts,
of rose beds and clipped lawns,
where I learnt to stitch on
that elastic tennis-club smile
to cover the slow dawning
that I was a Jew.

Self-Portraits and Life-Lines

EXERCISE 90: SELF-PORTRAIT ONE

In Inner Traits and Outside Influences you have Clustered a number of your traits, and should have a series of disconnected paragraphs. Now try building them into a continuous piece of prose to form a Self-Portrait. Here is a paragraph from a longer piece by a young man, followed by an extract from a piece by a young woman, one of John's students attending a workshop in prison:

Example One

'Timid' I have written down, 'Secretive', 'Outspoken' – how do the first two of these fit with the last? Well, I am certainly not physically courageous, and I tend to hug my feelings to myself. I suspect I have an ego that is easily bruised. But I am also a person of decided opinions. Take politics. I don't regard society as a free-for-all where the people who can grab the most should rise to the top of the pile. I feel affronted by those who must make-do on unacceptably low wages or try to get by on state benefits. And I stand up and say so in public meetings. I go to Union Meetings and argue the toss. It is as if having opinions somehow frees me from the shackles of my sensitive self. Where an argument is concerned I meet others on equal terms. I suppose, like most people, I'm rather a mixture of qualities . . .

Timothy Sandon

Example Two

An anger twists in my world, an anger that can make the towering inferno nothing but a flame. If I am pushed and my anger is awoken it can be dangerous, ugly and weird. Sometimes it is my defence mechanism, but what am I defending? What is so special within my world that I defend with such burning aggression?

It is probably my love. My love is a very deep emotion; it is deeper, truer and much more real than my anger. My love she rises with the sunset to meet with trust and friendship. Gold dulls considerably if my love stands next to it. My love is gentle and strong; she is young and vulnerable, yet old and wise. When my anger rears his head he rears up as a warrior with a sword and shield. He can cause pain in my world, the world he thinks he protects.

But my love, oh my sweet love, she rises quietly with a smile upon her lips, and a gently musical laughter shines from her large clear eyes. She rises with a sweet melody to mellow my world. Her slippers are made of loyalty.

There are many more characters alive and active in my world; there are also some that will be born in time. And others that have always been, but that I have failed to recognize so far. My world is good and bad; my world is strong and weak; my world is shallow and deep. I love my world. I hope you love yours.

EXERCISE 91: LIFE-LINE

Another method of building up a picture of yourself is the historical. A Life-Line is a diagram of your life upon which you have indicated some of the most significant events. Here is an example: Jane Birkett's charting of her first 21 years. When you have looked at it, draw your own Life-Line, or the Line of a significant part of your life, indicating the high and low points.

LIFE-LINE OF JANE BIRKETT

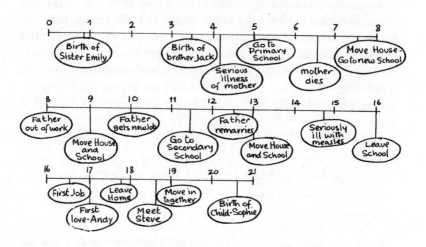

EXERCISE 92: THE HIGHSPOTS

All the events of our lives have a cumulative effect, serve collectively to make us into the unique individuals we are, but certain experiences have a vividness, for good or ill, which once enjoyed or endured are never forgotten, and at the deepest level mould us even against our wills. Here is the young Wordsworth out skating on the lake:

> When we had given our bodies to the wind,
> And all the shadowy banks, on either side,
> Came sweeping through the darkness, spinning still
> The rapid line of motion; then at once
> Have I, reclining back upon my heels
> Stopped short, yet still the solitary cliffs
> Wheeled by me, even as if the earth had roll'd
> With visible motion her diurnal round;
> Behind me did they stretch in solemn train
> Feebler and feebler, and I stood and watch'd
> Till all was tranquil as a dreamless sleep.

That was from *The Prelude*. It describes what was clearly a peak experience for Wordsworth, and one directly from Nature. Others, like his involvement in the French Revolution, were of ideals; or like his involvement with the leechgatherer in another poem, were of morality. Choose two or three of the most positive formative events of your life from your Life-Line to Cluster or Flow-Write, and develop pieces of writing from them. What strengths can you derive from what you have described? In what ways are you a better person from having lived through these experiences? Is there a sense of achievement stemming from your conduct which you have hitherto failed to value at its true worth?

EXERCISE 93: THE PROBLEM PAGES

We would now like you to give consideration to any entries on your Life-Line which you would consider times of crisis or difficulty. They might be events which provided a special challenge, or they might relate to any physical or mental handicaps which had to be endured or overcome. In Jane Birkett's case the death of her mother when Jane was six-and-a-half and the remarriage of her father when she was just into her teens would fall into the former category. By your chosen method of Clustering or Flow-Writing we invite you to focus upon any problem areas you feel able to write about.

The Australian poet Les Murray says that he was blocked from writing personal poems by two events: the death of his mother when he was 12, and his obesity which resulted in his victimization in the schools he attended, and which in turn caused what he describes as 'a profound sexual neurosis [. . .] I didn't know I was sick. I had two nervous breakdowns out of it. I think I've just about written it out now.' It was 30 years, though, before he felt able to tackle either of these areas. Turn to the Self-Image section of Themes and Examples to see one of his attempts to come to terms with this difficult area, in his poem 'Burning Want'.

It has frequently been observed that some experience of mental illness, often in the form of depression, comes to many people in modern society at some time in their lives. For the majority who are fortunate enough to survive it, this 'glance into the abyss' can play a constructive role in personality development. If an experience of an acute state features on your Life-Line, and you have also worked your way through the 'Techniques' part of this book, you may feel equipped to write about it at this juncture. We must stress, however, that this is a personal decision. If you feel that this course of action might lead to further instability in your life with which you would find difficulty in coping, then we would advise against it, certainly without the back-up of a therapist.

If you would be interested to read how various contemporary writers have dealt with crisis issues the book *Mind Readings: Writers' Journeys Through Mental States* can be recommended, with the provisos that some of the contributions are more interesting than others and it can be rather depressing to read so much material on the one theme.

EXERCISE 94: THE PATTERN OF LIVING

We are aware that the emphases on the highs and lows of existence that the drawing of a Life-Line necessarily entails ignore the fact that our lives are mostly filled with ordinary activities. A true Self-Portrait must surely take account of day-to-day existence. We suggest that in order to redress the balance you settle upon either one day or a week in your life to enumerate. There should be nothing special about the unit of time that you select. Draw a line resembling a Life-Line but marked off with hours or days rather than years. Write in the activities performed/how your time was spent. Now look at the pattern of your day or week. Which activities do you enjoy most and which must be endured? Can you account for this? Are you a person dominated by routine, or does spontaneity play a major part in your approach?

EXERCISE 95: SELF-PORTRAIT TWO

Now you are ready to make a second attempt at writing a Self-Portrait. This time your starting-point will be the events of your life rather than your perceived qualities. Look at the pieces of writing you have already produced for EXERCISE 92 and EXERCISE 93. How many more will you need before you have the basic material for a brief chronological account? After you have completed the necessary extra Clusterings and Flow-Writings assemble your pieces in the right order and add any linking passages. Make sure that you also take account of any insights thrown up by EXERCISE 94 about how you perform the minutiae of living.

Here is a paragraph from Jane Birkett's Self-Portrait:

When other people talk about their childhoods I want to hide away. Listening to them I think how happy they must have been. Probably they were not, but that's how they seem in comparison to me. Two events loom up like landmarks. I imagine myself as a ship, and either of these events could have sunk me. I only just survived. I don't know which hit me the harder. I suppose the loss of my mother was really the one to bring my world tumbling about my ears. After all, at six-and-a-half you are still a small child, and are quite unable to cope with an event of that magnitude. But then I was only twelve, and a very awkward adolescent, when a new woman (I could never bring myself to call her 'mother') entered my home and took control of my life. It was long after I had left school, after I had left home in fact, that I could begin to sort out exactly what sort of a person I was.

You have now completed two Self-Portraits. You may find it interesting to explore any points at which the accounts appear to be at variance – is this the result of faulty memory or judgement on your part (you are, after all, a very partial witness in these matters!) or is there a theme or relationship here that demands further exploration? Certainly if you have worked your way through the exercises of this section (not to mention those that preceded them) you will have amassed much material that would be of use if you were to go on to write a full-scale autobiography. A later section of the book deals with the challenges and problems of this major enterprise.

Part Four

Developing Pieces of Work

By the time you have reached this part of the book you are likely to have written about a number of topics and issues which you want to explore more deeply. You may also feel that some of your pieces of raw writing contain material which would work very well in a story, poem, rounded autobiographical piece, perhaps even in a play.

In this section we are going to look in detail at the ways in which seven people have developed their writing exercises or notes. There are, of course, no set ways to go about this – the possibilities are endless. However, we think these examples will offer a number of different ideas to draw on and give some valuable insights into the processes both of self-discovery and of writing.

One

Development from raw writing produced in an exercise or a note will probably involve some kind of expansion. The initial stage is, of course, extremely important. When a finished piece of writing seems thin and unsatisfying it is often because the writer didn't manage to record what really mattered to him/her in the first exercise or jottings. If you have set down material which excites you or seems mean-

ingful, memories, ideas and feelings are likely to surface
which will prompt you to take it further and straightforward
expansion is likely to follow easily.

In the following example Juanita Woolliscroft began with a
Tapping into Memory exercise about a place she remembered
which was significant to her:

> Until I was seven I lived in Taunton. Our house was in the
> outskirts of the town. It was wartime and the field outside
> our back gate was growing cabbages, enormous green cabbages
> almost as tall as I was with outer leaves chewed lacy by the
> caterpillars. Sometimes I collected the juicy green caterpillars in
> a jam jar. The damp pungent vegetable smell was overpowering.
> In summer to walk along the rows of cabbages was to walk in
> a cloud of white butterflies. At the entrance to the field stood a
> tractor where we children would play. Earth-coloured and
> warmed by the sun the metal felt smooth to the touch. The seat
> contoured to fit the shape of a man's bottom.
>
> Just outside the garden was a rough, stony piece of land bright
> with daisies and buttercups and tall feathery grasses. Often I
> poked about in the earth fantasising that I would one day create
> a magical garden. Sadly we left suddenly before my desire could
> be accomplished.

There is total recall of the cabbages and the child's world
with its possibility for magic. Juanita used this memory as a
starting point for a much longer autobiographical piece
which also began with a description of herself collecting
caterpillars in the cabbage field. Then her memories
expanded beyond the tractor to the country lanes along
which she walked to church and a piece of 'rich emerald
green' grass where she was convinced she would one morning
see something strange. This leads on to her reactions to the
church service.

She begins the next paragraph by saying she didn't realize
'the idyllic childhood years were drawing to a close' which
chimes with the final sentence of the exercise and this sense
of loss seems to underlie and heighten the memories. Juanita

goes on to describe, as part of the idyll, watching the planes, the Morrison shelter which to her was like a giant Wendy house, the fun of air-raids, and the excitement of the night when her father stood watching the planes from the door. The following morning her father wanted to locate the spot where a German plane had been shot down:

> Then we saw the cockpit, or what was left of it. It was only at this point that I really understood what had been going on. Still I imagined the pilot with his parachute floating safely down to earth. I felt he must have escaped or my father wouldn't have been so elated.
>
> 'But what happened to the pilot?' I asked, viewing the mangled wreckage. When he said that he must have been killed I was shocked and my father looking slightly embarrassed, explained: 'He was a German. It wasn't one of ours', as if that made it all right.
>
> Soon after that the war impinged on us even more closely. My father was sent abroad and my mother and sister and I left Taunton and went to live nearer some of our relatives. For a while it felt as if the bottom had dropped out of my world.

The exercise recalling the cabbage field prompted Juanita to describe her childhood world more fully in the second piece of writing. Significantly, this gave her the opportunity to explore how her idyllic life was eroded, first of all on the morning after the air raid when the plane wreckage and her father's attitude showed her what the War meant. She then pinpoints the greater shock of moving away from Taunton and losing her perfect world completely.

Two

In the next example the approach to expansion is different. Elke Dutton did a piece of Flow-Writing about silence and afterwards focused on a small part of it. Here is most of the Flow-Writing:

What is silence, I asked? Silence is a deep hole, velvet cushioned, black, smooth, mysterious. No dust, absolute. Quiet. It takes me to my inner self or being. In the silence, in the silence, why do I chatter so if silence is good. I dare not face myself. The self rises in the silence, the grieving self wells with tears, heaving, dissolving. Don't run away – watch, tell, observe. The bird that flutters on the branch is shot and splintered mindlessly on still afternoons, in silence. The child playing in the quiet dust is maimed and disfigured by a malevolent mortar shell.

A nebulous something that has a negative feel – links in the silence . . . I leave it for another day. Yet what is it we fear the most, the tiny child who could not sustain her very being without her mother – left to cope in a strange land, all alone. Strangers, strangers, who are these starchy strangers in white starched uniforms with bright smiles stitched onto their faces? Will they swoop down upon my messy face, food distributed in lumps about my mouth and wipe me with a harsh-smelling flannel? Will they stare with cold blue disapproving eyes at the contents of my nappy? Impossible to put the eiderdown on it no matter how hard I try.

Well, so now it might be better, instead of clamping down, damping down, stuffing my body with food to outweigh the panic left by unfaced fears from today and from the past – to lift the lid instead. What shall I find? Maggots crawling from dying bodies [. . .] emaciated birds mauled by cats, their thin stick wings coagulated in blood; so the bodies of Belsen and Auschwitz and Teresienstadt, creeping from place to place like beggars.

The first paragraph is a conflict between wanting to face the inner self and wanting to run away from its grief. The images of helpless beings suffering destruction are not related directly to the writer yet a connection is implied. In the second paragraph she deals with being abandoned and how she was treated by strangers. Interestingly the details are all put in the form of questions, a mode which continues the feeling of search. Also it is only in the middle of the paragraph that she switches from referring to 'the child' to writing

'my' and 'I' as if she'd been drawn far enough in to feel able
to identify herself.

In common with other quickly written exercises or notes
which contain powerful/significant material this piece of
spontaneous writing has a character, rhythm and quality
of its own. It is a moving example of struggling through
layers of resistance to uncover what is painful and appalling.
As such it is complete, a validation of the writer's experience
and we want to stress that developing a piece of work does
not mean rejecting the original. If one is going to develop an
exercise there should be a reason for doing so.

Elke's comments on her Flow-Writing make it very clear
why she wanted to develop it. She said that she was sent to
England from Czechoslovakia at the age of 14 months, just
before World War Two began. For the next few years she
lived in different places where she was cared for by strangers.
Later on she was re-united with her mother. She explained
that she has no memory of her first seven years apart from
one or two fragments like lying in bed and not wanting to
leave it. She also explained that she used writing to create a
childhood for herself. Having 'found' or 'allowed' the child
in the Flow-Writing, Elke expanded the part about her early
life, drawing on fragments she remembered and making up
details that were likely to be true.

Here is the poem she wrote:

Among Strangers

Who are these white strangers
Upright in starched aprons,
Flannels ready in scrubbed hands,
With bright smiles stitched onto their faces,
Their blue eyes fixed on messes
Round her mouth, their noses held
Against her leaking smell?

A white porcelain bath stands
Antiseptic on a wooden floor.

> Thin fingers turn the tap,
> Measure out the lukewarm water.
> She climbs into a brief assault
> Of yellow soap, then shivers, thankful
> for release to a coarse towel.
>
> Black shadows creep around
> Rows of creaking metal beds.
> Humped beneath two grey blankets
> She thrusts her knees towards her damp breath,
> Clamps her arms tight against her flesh.
> At last her urine seeps out
> Warm, familiar, spreading into sleep.

In the first stanza she keeps the searching, questioning form but then moves to direct statement. Writing in the third person frees her from sticking to the fragments of fact. Need, imagination and practice in writing have helped her to produce descriptions which are immediate and convincing with their precise visual and tactile details. Especially moving is the end, the way in which the isolated child finds comfort and release. Technically, the poem is more controlled than the Flow-Writing and because the childhood is realized in greater detail it is more fully validated.

Three

Peter Newton wrote about a childhood memory. He began to turn this into a story which surprised him by taking off in a direction he had not at all intended. The raw writing was triggered by a photograph of stubble burning:

> Below the thick black smoke were violent flames with dark blue roots. If we didn't hurry the whole field would be burning and the trees beyond . . . there would be a forest fire no one could quench. 'Take those beaters,' I ordered Jim, pointing at some hefty sticks lying by the hedge, 'and stamp out the flames.' We struck again and again, didn't give up even though our arms

ached and our eyes stung and we kept coughing. We'd more or
less won when we saw two men at the far end of the field. They
were waving and shouting angrily. We ran away. I told Jim
they were the enemy, the ones that started the fire.

'We're heroes,' said Jim when Mum let us in.

'You're a pair of ninnies,' she interrupted almost as soon as I
launched into a description of our triumph. 'Farmers always
burn stubble. Look at the mess you're both in and really, Peter,
you're nearly eleven. You're too old for this kind of fantasy.'

In the bath I twisted a sponge with fury. I'd show her, one
day I'd show her.

His mother's reaction and the description of the fire gave
Peter the idea of writing a story about Jake, a 16-year-old
daydreamer who was constantly criticized by his parents.
He'd planned to make Jake's fantasies increasingly outrageous, funny even, until he accidentally won approbation
for something that seemed trivial to him. Here is an extract
from the draft:

Ignoring the voices calling him back, Jake ran inside. Coughing
and flailing his arms he pushed through the smoke. Somehow he
reached the cot, grabbed the small whimpering bundle, hugged it
against his chest. More than anything else in the world he had
ever desired he wanted to keep it alive. As he turned to retreat
he began to choke. Something heavy cracked and fell behind
him. Terrified, he bent his knees and staggered towards the door.
He had a sense of gulping, of faces, of delivering the baby into
arms. Then he was pulled into darkness.

He was in a hospital bed, arms, hands, face bandaged. Mum
was silent, a look of awed admiration on her face. A nurse, fair-
haired, beautiful was saying: 'He risked his life; he's a hero.' She
looked into his eyes and he knew . . .

Jake was now on a platform, 'For outstanding bravery'. He
was shaking hands with Martin Milder, the famous television
presenter. Below, rows of people were clapping. Among them
the nurse, Jeanette, still gazing, the baby's grateful parents and
both his parents beaming, proud . . . He wanted to go on looking
at his parents' faces, at Jeanette, but they faded and were

replaced by his house. He was outside it in the cold. Driven by a terrible anger he was emptying a can of petrol on rolled-up sheets of newspaper he'd placed by the door and against the walls. That would teach them, a voice in his head kept saying . . .

At this point Peter stopped the draft, shaken by an image of himself as an arsonist. A few days later he noted in his journal:

That last image forced its way in – was writing about myself, of course – my role in the family!! I was shocked by how great my anger still is with Ma and Pa – for all those years of cutting me down to size. I went into the adult world feeling useless, a worm. No way the two doddery old things would ever understand how they trod on me. Last night wrote a letter to them blasting them for unmanning me. Then I tore it up and burnt it in the garden. I nearly threw the story away but will re-do it, make it highlight Jake's anger, show him breaking out of his strait-jacket, show in a dramatic way what I only did late and slowly and am still recognizing NOW. Need to re-structure the plot, get rid of the juvenile hospital scene and the baby-rescuing bit which seems to want to be about feelings of struggle rather than a heroic daydream.

Peter's fiction surprised him into expressing feelings of anger with his parents that he is still coming to terms with. The image which surfaced was so strong it interrupted the story. He released some of his rage in his Secret Letter and then he examined it more rationally in his journal. This example shows how writing can lead to self-discovery, also how helpful the fictional form can be in uncovering painful feelings. The rescuing of the baby has the quality of an Image Exploration and Peter was struck by the feelings underlying it. When he develops the story it will probably have a more subtle plot than the one he originally planned and, whether it is in the form of fantasy or not, it is likely to have a theme which is important to him.

Four

The next example shows how writing helped Jill Bamber cope with her feelings during her ex-husband's last illness and after his death. She began with a series of exercises, the first of which was Clustering using the word 'tunnel'. Here is the diagram:

The different strands in this Cluster list many ways of being cut off and also reflect a fear of death. Jill commented that any exercise at that time would have led her to the same subject. With the Cluster diagram in front of her she wrote a spontaneous poem in the sharp voice of her husband, ill and isolated by his disabilities, trapped in the 'tunnel of kindness'. The poem also shows how closely she identified with his feelings of alienation and anger. Here is part of it:

Bed-Rest

Who are you?
Take your hands off me now!
I can still throw this cup
one-handed. Once more
and I'll bite you.
Just try me. I gave
no permission to stay.
I'll ring the police
if you put me in nappies again.
You're just out of school.
Do you know what it means
to be me? Lay off me!
You press on my heels
and another thing,
where are my batteries?
I can't hear a thing
in this tunnel of kindness.
You know I can't see . . .

Later, with the 'Tunnel' Cluster still in mind, Jill expressed in a piece of Flow-Writing her longing to help, to make connection and also her fear. This is quoted as an example to EXERCISE 11 in Part Two: Flow-Writing. The stop and start, mix of single words, questions, long running sentences echo her state of mind. She also used Dorothy Nimmo's poem 'Dream Play' (see Part Two: Modelling, EXERCISE 21) as a model for writing another monologue in her ex-husband's voice. This incorporated many of the phrases from the piece of Flow-Writing and shows how she felt he saw her.

In the following months Jill wrote a long journal entry, part of which is included in EXERCISE 100 in Part Five: Keeping a Journal, and three poems. In the first poem, 'Anchor and Chain', she expresses some of her feelings and thoughts in descriptions of gulls flying but the poem is not fully focused. The second poem, 'Sweet Thames Run Softly', is about a visit Jill made to the home which was caring for her ex-husband. Some of its material comes from her exercises. It examines her ambivalences more fully and includes powerful new descriptions like this in the second stanza:

> But I can't divorce cancer.
> The white rosette he wears
> is still my necklace.
> His shoulders poke
> like old umbrella struts.

The third poem, 'Brailling the Sheet', went through many drafts. Here it is:

> You sit and stare at sun that would blind me.
> I draw the curtains over the centre of dazzle.
> 'You know nothing,' you say. 'I can see colours
> dance behind my eye-lids,' shutting
> me out, bolting the doors of your blindness.
>
> I know you are dying. Maybe six months,
> the doctor said. Cancer is lawless.
> It throws a noose around your neck, strangles
> the talking. Your practised hands forget
> to braille the life-long diary.
>
> I didn't know your bones would stand out so,
> a negative emblazoned on the sheet.
> I could blow you away or keep you
> like the Turin shroud, proved genuine,
> repeating in the faces of our children.
>
> 'This is my wife,' you say, annulling divorce.
> Last night you fell and they found you
> on one of their rounds. 'Which side of the bed
> do you lie on?' I ask, knowing full well.
> 'Have you forgotten?' you say, 'two halves of a shell.'
>
> I remember the first time we kissed
> climbing the Downs on the Wilmington Long-man
> with his two white sticks, holding hands,

slipping on flints, your hair as pale
as the bleached grass on the side of the hill.

The 'Talking Clock' ticks like a bomb on the locker.
'This isn't my bed,' you say. Better than knowing
everything hurts. They are letting you go,
a broken doll, lying askew. It won't be long
before they lay you straight.

The opening lines, also stanzas two and three incorporate
material from 'Anchor and Chain' and there are other details
which can be traced back to the first exercises and poems.
The writing still conveys the sense of shock and the pain but
the whole experience is more crystallized. The relationship is
looked at more directly and there is a dramatic and poignant
memory of the past. Each of the earlier pieces offers a perspective which is not found elsewhere, each is moving in its
own particular way, the cry and anger in the monologue
'Bed-Rest', the grief and longing in the Flow-Writing, for
example. But in the extension of its ideas, its powerful
imagery and convincing form 'Brailling The Sheet' is the
most fully realized.

Five

When Elke Dutton read through her piece of Flow-Writing
beginning: 'What is silence', she knew exactly which part of
it she wanted to expand into a poem. Sometimes, however,
we produce pieces of raw writing and it is difficult to decide
which of the ideas to use or to work out how best to develop
the material. We are now going to look at what happened
when Myra wrote a poem drawing on two connected pieces
of Flow-Writing which excited her. Here are relevant extracts
from the exercises:

First Extract

That moment when the ground, the floor, the chair, the cushion – buildings, roads, my stomach, my body lose their substance. Stones crack, roads break up; beneath me only shifting vapoury layers. Strength siphoned off. My voice, my whole being carries no weight. There is nowhere safe. I am fragmented. I cannot hold onto my core and the Critical Voice is shouting: 'You ought to be able to cope. You're not a child, you are nearly an old woman.' I am scrabbling, a flake of leaf on a ledge [. . .]

I am torn into small pieces, destroyed and distraught until anger begins to solidify me. Then I find footing and turn round and look at the truth of where I am. There is no need to raise my voice. I hear it now, see how far I've taken myself [. . .]

I can hear now, bell-clear, the other voices I've found and the fierce red joy, and my toes touch waterbird rings on lake calm; inside me the lapping of harp music.

Second Extract

Terror that the huge voice outside will swallow me whole, that I will be torn into shreds of paper, dust, that I will be nothing in my own right [. . .] And yet if I hold tight, summon up even a smattering of courage, turn a few degrees the huge figures begin to shrink and I begin to gain weight [. . .] and although I am afraid I can look the panic bird in its terrible eye and although my voice trembles I answer it back and it begins to let go of its hold on my neck.

In these pieces the 'flow' took Myra to her inner self, its different voices and in particular the fearful voice remaining from her childhood. The second piece was written five weeks after the first and when she looked at them together she was struck by the description in both of the crushing of the weak self and the way it re-asserted itself, also by the opening of the first piece, its rhythm and energy. She assumed that if she tried to translate this from prose to poetry or write an equivalent it would lose its force. She was also impressed by the introduction of the word 'panic bird' at the end of the second piece. She decided to focus on the different inner

voices including a reasonable adult voice to which she gave
the name of 'referee' though it hardly had a presence in the
exercises. She wrote a poem called 'The Voices'. Here is part
of it:

> The voices are all competing
> for my attention, know nothing
> about living together, team spirit.
> Some, I suspect, are infiltrators –
> don't belong to me at all.

> The referee is hanging back
> in an anonymous mack, speaking
> in whispers, letting the critic
> rout confidence and calm.
> She only offers decisive words,
> a supportive arm, her clear vision
> of the way forward, to others.

> I want a voice that will outshout
> the strutter, its never-ending:
> 'you ought . . . omitted . . . caused
> offence . . . committed a deadly sin,'
> and power to shut the rock-blue eyes,
> tear off its gaudy feathers,
> nail the merciless judge,
> mother/father tyrant,
> the body inflated by panic.

Uncertain about the poem and its loose form, Myra discussed
it with a perceptive friend. It soon became clear that she had
tried to expand too many of the ideas and images in the
Flow-Writing. As a result the beginning was too explanatory
and the poem only seemed to come to life when the panic
bird entered in the third stanza. She re-read the Flow-Writing
and this confirmed what her friend was suggesting, that the
panic bird was at the heart of the poem. In fact, the whole
poem needed to progress towards the idea of defeating the

panic bird with a suggestion at the end that it is transformed into a waterbird.

Changing tack and cutting can be difficult in developing work but it is essential to be prepared to do either or both. In this case much of the material about the competing inner voices was discarded, but put in a folder, maybe to be used elsewhere. As she began the revision the opening words of the first exercise presented themselves to Myra in a poetic rhythm. Using these and the panic bird idea she gave the poem a new opening and wrote the first part of it in four stanzas, each with five short lines, leaving the rest of it in the original shape. Finally, she took the bull by the horns and fined down all the material to fit it into the same form, turning the poem into a dramatic inner narrative:

The Panic Bird

That moment
when the mattress splits
and seeps its stuffing
when floors crack, roads
break up, ground gapes

that moment
when the breathstream
dries, the belly ceases
to exist and the self
can no longer hold on

that moment
when reason bolts
and six obsessive words
pound pound on the shell
of the emptied brain

is the moment
the wingspan spreads.
The predator descends
traps hair, neck –
I am eclipsed.

I try to yell
for someone to put out
the rock-blue eyes,
smash the razor beak,
crush the claws.

Only a child
looms. Weightless as a leaf
she's crouched on a mountain ledge
whimpering: 'I can't bear
blood, illness, change.'

I want to
take her in my arms, struggle
to a safe place, outstare
the bird, seize it by the neck,
pull the gaudy feathers.

I want to
call out, voice belled
by fierce red joy, to alight
toes touching waterbird
rings on lake calm.

Six

We are now going to look at three exercises done on the
same writing day by Heather Seddon and how she later drew
on them. The first was Flow-Writing. As a lead in she'd been
asked to list some objects which were sharp and jot down
an associated feeling. Heather listed: 'Razor, scissors,
grassblade' and 'danger'. 'A long way down' was then given
as an opening for the Flow-Writing. Here is a key section:

A long way down she fell and the landing was a pit of knives.
The only consolation that there was no further descent and there
in the pit was knowledge of a sort, if only of the ultimate
vulnerability of the self that is the end we come to once we let
ourselves fall, so generally we don't fall into the void – rather
keep walking on the air.

The next exercise was to write about a possession. Heather described a slide rule. This led her to a memory and brought up the question of masculinity/femininity. She underlined this paragraph:

> I remember maths when two places of decimals weren't good enough, partly because our teachers thought it was cheating not to slog through the four figure tables, and physics and chemistry where often enough it would do. The smell of old wooden benches and sharp chemicals and the constant struggle to make acceptable sense of what looked like just another fine mess of something coagulated in the bottom of a test tube or a long list of readings [. . .] it (the slide rule) was a present from my father, a kind of passport to the world of science, engineering, out of the clinging amorphous emotional feminine world.

The third exercise was an Image Exploration. Heather's piece describes a cold, unused room that seemed just to have been opened and the appearance of an imposing woman. Here is the dialogue at the end:

> I had a sense of standing on someone's holy ground.
> 'If I'm in the way I could wait outside,' I said.
> 'What is the true measure?' She had a deep commanding voice.
> The true measure of what? I wondered.
> 'What is the length of a day?' She pulled out the steel tape with a metallic whisper. 'How many inches do the flowers live?' She pointed the waving end of the measure at the dead dandelions.
> 'Shall I wait in the corridor?'
> She turned on me and spoke directly. 'How shall we live without a measure of our lives? How? Tell me how?'
> 'I – I don't know.' The tape measure was wavering in front of my face.

This piece has a very Alice-in-Wonderland feel in its logic and some of its imagery connects directly with the previous exercise. Heather commented that the woman appears to be asking an important question but it is a stereotypically masculine question, the attempt to quantify life. In the three pieces Heather seems to be trying to assess where she is in life, maybe face underlying problems.

Much of the material that surfaced in this raw writing was used in drafting a chapter of a novel she was writing at the time. Woven into the train of thought of Isabel, the main character, it is related directly to her past, the danger she is in and her inner turmoil. The questioning and assessing of life is taken further than in the exercises and the tone is more urgent. We quote two relevant extracts. In the first Isabel is considering her life at a moment of outer and inner crisis:

> What is the true measure? The measure of a life? Not in years alone, that she knew. Old age is not in itself a virtue. Can you measure a year well spent against a year wasted? Or four years wasted? And how would you know? There must be some yard-stick, some point of reference. Or how is anything to be measured? How shall we judge ourselves?
>
> The flowers that Eva had brought her three days ago, without explanation, leaving her to wonder if it was an offer of reconcili-ation or a gesture of dismissal, the flowers had drooped already and were dying. What was the measure of their life? To what end had they bloomed and withered, fruitless on the stem? Isabel had kicked off her shoes in a temper the second she'd slammed her door and now she walked feverishly back and forth over the chill hard tiles.

And later when the tension becomes unbearable:

> Her nerves were in shreds, her resistance withering. If the soldiers came back she would break down and tell them everything. She would fall into their hands [. . .] into the dark.
>
> The terrace was tilting towards her. She felt herself sliding off into blackness. A long way down she fell onto a bed of knives that flickered like flames while beneath her moved great subter-ranean tides, cold and unfathomable. She was calmly aware that she would die here, would bleed to death and the waters would swallow up her blood without trace and her body would wither

and dry and fall away from the cold transfixing iron and be dust, and the waters would carry her dust away.

And there was no measure at all.

The dramatic 'falling down' now relates to obliteration, pointlessness.

Heather's own comments on this draft and her exercises are revealing:

> I can't remember just how much idea I had about the chapter that this eventually became but I think it was this material that really gave it the direction and drive even though the characters and to some·extent the events were already there.
>
> As for the question of self-discovery, the conflict between the feminine and masculine spheres of life, the issue of how you judge your own life and, if you feel your life to be unsuccessful or unfulfilled, the constant fear of falling combined with the temptation to let it happen, are all my own concerns. It was, of course, easier to use Isabel to express some of them in her way.

It is worth noting how the personal/inner material was woven into an already existing plot giving it a stronger purpose. Heather's points are also a reminder that many writers feel they can explore their ideas and feelings much more freely in fiction.

Seven

We are going to end this section by looking at notes and a poem by William Ayot who evolved his own method of writing, after attending a workshop where he heard about a writer who found it possible to write a poem every morning because he didn't worry about what standard the poem reached. William found the story useful because it made him realize the extent to which he had been blocked by the idea of perfectionism. He commented: 'It was Keats or nothing, the result, of course, being nothing.' Here is William's description of the technique he devised:

> I decided to write down my first thoughts each morning. Because of what was going on with me at the time a lot of powerful stuff came up but after a while things dried up again so I evolved this strategy for getting back to the threshold of my dreams. When I wake up I take my pad and lay it on my bed. I then try to resume the position I was sleeping in and, if possible, make my way back into the dream images that were current before I woke up. I then write down the images. If I can't do that I just allow myself to write any thoughts and feelings. When I feel I'm losing the flow I sit up and write a poem – no matter how stupid, scary, sexual or whatever. The important thing for me is to overcome my self-consciousness and to do it – eat the peach.
>
> I found, doing this, that I was freeing up stuff that I had wanted to write but that my internal critic had previously censored as soon as it surfaced. 'Dangerous' subject matter turned out to be less dangerous on the page and by recovering my dreams I was soon getting in touch with long-forgotten events and the feelings around them.

William's method connects very much with Flow-Writing, also with ways we have suggested for writing about dreams and keeping a journal. It may be something you would like to try out. You may also might want to try out methods of your own for producing raw material and developing writing. It is also well worth experimenting with the times/ places that are best for you to work.

Now let us look at a set of notes William wrote over two or three early morning sessions:

> Remembrance Sunday. Duty. The Old Boys of the village [where he grew up] telling me about the Great War. Passchendael, Ypres. Mud in their mouths. Tears on the drum.
>
> Whole villages of men dying on the same morning. Young, afraid – *walking* into battle. They understood (Do I?) that dying is what you do.
>
> It's expected. It's what men are for.

A Guatemalan/Mayan rhythm that Martin uses in rituals. A Responsum.

Now I know/How these men/Young and afraid/Could rise up swearing/With mud in their mouths/And tears on the drum. [William explained that Martin, who was on a course he attended, spoke in these rhythms.]

Q: Is that why the Old Boys always cried when they told their stories?

David and I should have been able to cry on each other's shoulders but we couldn't and now he's dead. There was never the time anyway. [David was a very close friend and took the place of a brother as William doesn't have one.] Still a lot of grieving to do here – seems to be a part of life now.

'Women and Children First'

Men going down with the ship, waving at the boats. That troop-ship sinking off the coast of Africa (The *Victoria*?) the men holding hands and singing hymns as it went down.

The orchestra on the *Titanic*. The millionaire John Jacob Astor sharing a joke with someone, then shaking his hand and *walking* down into the water.

It's not just melodramatic heroism – there's something fundamentally male here – mature male. It's what's expected again – it's a given.

William talked to Myra about the areas of interest in these notes: his need to get in touch with his past and himself, that is his spiritual self, other side or 'brother' – something he has been doing in recent years, and in conjunction with this, the way men are conditioned not to show their feelings. This male behaviour was very much in his mind when he listened to the stories of the Great War and thought about the troop ship and the *Titanic* going down.

Here is the compact poem that arose from the notes and a dream:

Tears on the Drum

We are standing together, my long-lost brother and I,
On the sloping deck of a holed and dying luxury liner.

We are sharing a fine cigar because we have no jokes.
He is talking about the Grandfathers who went before.

Today I understand how these young men,
Lonely and afraid, could rise up smiling
In far-off, strange, unhallowed places
With mud on their tongues and tears on the drum;

How they could gather, to pick sweet poppies,
The red, red poppies, and when they were gathered,
To walk together, into the morning,
The misty morning, and die together.

We need to weep awhile, my long-lost brother and I
But we both know the score – there's never the time.
So we wave once more at the distant boats. Then
We smile, hold hands, and walk down into the water.

The first stanza of this poem is a vision from a dream which
William had one night after he had written the notes. The
second and third stanzas use the Guatemalan/Mayan rhythm
he mentioned in the notes. In the last stanza he is thinking
both of his spiritual self and of his dead friend. The poem
has an extraordinary sense of compassion. It's both an elegy
and a crystallization of self-discovery.

In addition to the work we have surveyed in this section
John describes in detail the methods he used to produce new
material from remembered fragments of dreams and quotes
the poems he developed. You may want to look at this
material again. It is in Part Two: Dreams and Active Imagin-
ings. We hope that the various possibilities that we have
shown in our examples will inspire you to be daring, inventive and persistent as you develop your own work.

PART FIVE
Journals and Autobiographies

Keeping a Journal

In this section we are going to consider the creative diary, not the kind which is a factual record of the day's main events with the addition of a few comments. What we have in mind is a journal in which one notes down thoughts, feelings, sudden illuminations, writes entries about people and their behaviour, places, books, problems, decisions, key events, small pleasures – anything that excites, anything that matters. Such a journal allows its writer to explore his/her outer and inner worlds freely, a process that leads to insights, new ideas. It is an invaluable resource in writing for self-discovery, for any kind of writing.

Anne Frank's famous diary is very readable because the entries are so immediate. The reader is drawn straight into the cramped rooms where two families and a dentist lived in hiding, their fears, food shortages, quarrels, Anne's turbulent feelings, her growing awareness of sex and self and the spirit with which she held onto a belief in life:

> This is one of the things that Mummy and I are so entirely different about. Her counsel when one feels melancholy is: 'Think of all the misery in the world and be thankful that you are not sharing it!' My advice is: 'Go outside, to the fields, enjoy nature and the sunshine, go out and try to recapture happiness

in yourself, in God. Think of all the beauty that's still left in and around you and be happy!'

This diary, written in the form of letters to an imaginary and understanding friend, gave Anne the freedom to be herself in circumstances where this was particularly difficult to achieve.

Support is often a function of the journal. In Part Six: Life Stages we quote from the diary Anne Tibble kept for seven years after her husband died. In it she addressed him directly and this method of keeping in touch with him enabled her to come to terms with losing him. The Scottish poet William Soutar who suffered ill-health for much of his adult life, kept a dream diary for years and an ordinary journal sporadically. In July 1943 after he'd been told he only had a limited time to live he headed an exercise book: *The Diary of A Dying Man* and wrote in this secretly for the remaining three months of his life. It is witty, contemplative, full of observations about the people who visit him, makes detached comments about his physical state and behaviour with resolutions to control his irritability and not to give way to weakness.

Many journals have a particular slant. Gerard Manley-Hopkins used his journal and notebook mainly to make detailed descriptions of nature in which he was passionately interested. Even when he came to the conclusion that it was impossible for him to remain in the Church of England (a realization which he must have known would affect his relationship with his family as well as the direction of his life) it only appears as a brief reference.

Poet Mimi Khalvati keeps a book in which she writes down ideas, drafts, notes. Here is the main part of an entry:

Whenever I wake from dreams of people I know that capture their essence, I recall being told, or reading: *remember whoever you dream of is you, a part of you* and I always baulk at the truth of this, for it was *you* I dreamt of, *you* and *you*, more than you were in life obscured by my presence.

Exactly the way I told people in a workshop I'd given a poem to translate, in scripts they couldn't read (Farsi, Yiddish), after they'd written their 'translation', that it wasn't one at all but a poem as surely in their own voice, part of that voice, as what they thought of their own voice as – since by this time, having produced poems utterly unlike their normal sort of thing, they were somehow convinced this was because they were indeed 'translations'.

I told them this, knowing it wasn't true – any more than people I dream of not being themselves but *me* isn't true – knowing that something had jumped from the script into their soul and lodged there.

Myra keeps a notebook which is mainly a store cupboard for writing. It contains collections of notes for poems, occasional references to pivotal events and her inner self. She also includes descriptions and fragments such as 'dragonflies were on the planet long before dinosaurs' and her son saying 'I could kill for aubergines'. Some of these find their way into poems.

In recent years there has been a great interest in keeping a diary which concentrates on exploring inner life and personal development. You may want to keep this kind of journal and if you do we suggest you read *The New Diary* by Tristine Rainer which offers many ideas, useful advice and is very balanced in its approach.

Some people are great letter writers, express their thoughts and feelings to friends, lovers or close relatives in the kind of detail that makes their letters very much like journal entries. Well-known letter writers include Keats, Van Gogh, Wilfred Owen, Elizabeth Bishop, Katherine Mansfield. If you write frankly and fully to anyone it might be a good idea to include your letters in your journal or even to make these its basis.

You may well have clear ideas about the kind of journal you want to keep but, if you are uncertain, the following exercises should help you to sort out your thoughts and make a start. They may also be useful if you want to extend the ways in which you are using a journal you are already writing.

EXERCISE 96

The first part of this exercise is the same as At This Moment, EXERCISE 1. It is a very good way of starting a journal because it makes you focus on what is happening to you now both externally and internally. Begin then just as you did in that very first exercise by describing a few objects – a piece of furniture, a dried up plant, an unsorted pile of letters and leaflets, a bowl of fruit, a stain on the wall, a half-eaten piece of toast, etc – things that catch your attention in the room or place you are in, also anything you are aware of outside. Be sure to note what you can hear and smell, also the texture of something close enough to touch. Write briefly about your feelings and then go straight onto the second stage of this exercise which is to Flow-Write for a few minutes. If you need a prompt to make the change, choose a word or phrase from what you have written so far. Use this to write the first sentence that comes into your head and then carry on writing whatever suggests itself. This may well take you far from your initial description but should raise material which matters to you at this moment.

EXERCISE 97

Write down the first details or feelings that come into your head about a recent key event, piece of news, moving book, bad day, amusing incident, etc, and let yourself take off in Flow-Writing.

Example

I'm so afraid I'll feel trapped down there and not able to leave. Michael is a bit too pessimistic – he's so steeped in statistics but it's my father we're talking about, not a number on a graph. He's always been very strong, very fit. I don't want to know about the odds stacked against him. No one can live without hope.

Claustrophobia, clock ticking, shopping, Auntie Winnie. Boring. Anxiety. Can I cope? Will I be too exhausted to look after two elderly parents? Head in the sand. He doesn't believe he won't be able to look after himself after the operation.

Panic rising. Holiday – selfish, am I being selfish? Dutiful daughters – Victorian concept. Piano legs covered up black – black hearse – coffin pulled by sleek black horses – mourning black veils – duty – discipline – no fun on Sundays spent going to church – no games, religious books and the Bible, trapped, repressed.

Juanita Woolliscroft

In this piece Juanita has let herself write what surfaced about her anxiety and conflict together with memories. The free association, use of short staccato sentences, the move into notes has helped her to follow her shifts in thought and her mixture of feelings. Had she stopped to sort and explain everything she would have been less likely to have caught her different feelings or the set of visual images and ideas from the past which have connections – especially in words like 'duty' and 'trapped' – with her present feelings. As it is the writing is very alive and a real reflection of her state of mind.

EXERCISE 98

There is another way of releasing feelings which is very useful if you find it difficult to 'let go', can't pinpoint your mood or if you have a number of emotions all fighting for your attention. This is simply to list in any order all the feelings you are aware of. You can state each one or relate it to its context – whatever feels right as you go along.

Example

I've been exhausted all day.
I'm irritable.
I resent the people in the flat downstairs.
I'm bloody fed up with the pressures at work.
I'm sick of the demands people put on me.
I hate my mother's emotional blackmail.
I feel guilty for telling her I had to work last Sunday and
   couldn't go to see her.
I'd like to spend a week lying in bed reading.
I want someone to listen to *me* for at least an hour.
In spite of knowing lots of people I feel very alone.
Uplifted by listening to Mahler's Resurrection symphony.

Robert Standing

Separating a bunch of stressful feelings and crystallizing them by writing them down can greatly ease tension. For a person under pressure this may be sufficient for the time being. Robert could also use the list as a starting point and go on to do any or all of these:

1. Explaining his resentment of the people downstairs.
2. Examining his feelings about his mother and looking back over the relationship.
3. Thinking how he could find more space for himself and what he would like to do with it.
4. Clustering or Flow-Writing about his sense of loneliness and his relationships with other people.
5. Describing the Mahler symphony and its effect on him.
6. Noting down ideas for tackling his main problems.

EXERCISE 99

A strong reason for keeping any kind of journal is the desire to record and describe things one doesn't want to forget. This is a positive expression of living and it plays a part in the process of self-discovery through writing. A detailed account of a visit to a botanical garden in Madeira, a note about a comedian you saw live who made you double up with laughter, a paragraph explaining what moved you in Toni Morrison's novel *Beloved*, a humorous description of a cricket match you played in, a series of images about an illuminating moment – any of these that interest you so much that you want to spend time writing about them, are part of the fabric that make up you, your life. Experiment with writing short and longer descriptions of views that strike you, incidents you've particularly enjoyed, paintings, books or films that have moved you or made you think, people you have watched or had contact with briefly and small happenings catching telling details and sensations.

Here's a description from Katherine Mansfield's journal. It was written at a villa at Menton on the French-Italian border in 1920 and headed 'Breakfast Time'.

> It grew hot. Everywhere the light quivered green-gold. The white soft road unrolled, with plane-trees casting a trembling shade. There were piles of pumpkins and gourds: outside the house the tomatoes were spread in the sun. Blue flowers and red flowers and tufts of deep purple flared in the road-side hedges. A young boy, carrying a branch, stumbled across a yellow field, followed by a brown high-stepping little goat. We bought figs for breakfast, immense thin-skinned ones. They broke in one's fingers and tasted of wine and honey. Why is the northern fig such a chaste fair-haired virgin, such a soprano? The melting contraltos sing through the ages.

Anne Morrow Lindbergh (wife of Lindbergh, the aviator) found her own way of using description as a starting point. In mid-life she went on holiday by the sea to have some space for herself. While away she began keeping a journal and started each entry with a description of a shell which she used as a lead-in for contemplating herself and where she was at in life. Try describing an object that is meaningful to you, or a series of objects, as a way into writing about aspects of your life.

EXERCISE 100

Many diary entries, of course, are a mixture of descriptions, comments, records of feelings and thoughts, memories, questionings and problems. Entries in an individual diary may vary greatly in length and frequency. Jill Bamber writes two or three detailed entries a month, very often to relieve her feelings. She also finds it comforting to look back and re-read her entries. We include part of a December diary entry. This connects with her exercises and poems about her ex-husband which we examined in Part Four: Developing Pieces of Work.

> I couldn't put up a tree. The golden stars are still folded flat in their box. The house is full of the smell of him, bags of his clothes to be taken to Oxfam. It's the sweetish smell of Daz and it fills me. I've kept the canary yellow towelling robe. It's so clean . . .
>
> I keep away from the cellar. Water seeps up from the ground. Perhaps it's the water table rising. There's a small depression in the corner and it spreads along a crack and under the tea-crates. 'Better raise them on bricks,' I said to Christopher [her son]. 'Don't worry,' he says but somebody has to. I'll smell mould and it'll be too late then. It'll be me fetching bricks from the stone-masons, the one in the High Road next to the cemetery. I'm still waiting for him to clear away the dead, twisted tomato vines from the trellis. I'm sure they harbour disease. 'On a fine day,' he says . . .
>
> The navvy has wings of long red hair and is bald on top. His brand new Yamaha reclines at the kerb girdled with a chain encased in clear yellow plastic like a shining plait. He has no idea why the house is filled with a sweetish smell or why there are no golden stars hanging in the hall [. . .]
>
> I keep dreaming of him: that we are travelling, climbing up and down stairs and ledges, Filey Brigg, the cliffs in Guernsey.

Somehow we're in the garden at Upland, young and in love. Speed bonny boat. When there's an itch in my back I can scratch it. He couldn't, couldn't stand, couldn't sit, couldn't anything. Nowhere was comfortable. He just endured inside himself.

At least I don't have to agonize for him any more. The hall is full of men's muddy shoes, while they walk through in socks. The navvy wears pink ones. He goes outside to smoke a roll-up.

I must send a card to Pete, Don's best and last friend who told me Don was overjoyed that I was coming to see him after so long but how could I have gone sooner when Doris was alive and still so jealous? She must have bought him the canary-coloured robe.

In this piece the descriptions of the hall and the cellar carry and echo Jill's grief. The memories and the dream relay the jumble of feelings, her sense of dislocation.

Try writing a very full diary entry round an event or situation which is important to you. Include descriptions, your feelings, memories and any other thoughts or connections that occur to you. In the context of a full entry you may find you can write about matters you can't talk about, matters that are even difficult to think about, eg feelings of overwhelming anger with your child, hatred of your boss, a sense of inadequacy, a phobia, a disturbing perception about the way someone has treated you, an aspect of your own behaviour you feel ashamed of.

Don't feel the *only* way to tackle problematic material is to explain and analyse it. Not only may this be painful, it does not necessarily lead to full investigation. With difficult or complex subject matter try using one or more of the techniques we have introduced in this book. Secret Letters and Dialogues may be useful in writing about situations closely connected with other people. Internal Dialogues, Image Exploration and Modelling may help you if you are trying to focus on your inner feelings and thoughts. Clustering is well worth trying if you are exploring an issue with several different strands to it. Flow-Writing and Drawing (diagrams) may be helpful in any kind of exploration.

It is also worth thinking about balancing positive and negative. If you find your diary entries tend to concentrate on unhappy experiences, make yourself include some descriptions of moments or events you have enjoyed. If you find you are always criticizing yourself, start an entry with a list of your qualities and then write about one of them. If your journal tends to be a series of descriptions of beautiful views and enjoyable outings with friends, try relating an incident or conversation during which you had some uncomfortable feelings.

Most important of all your diary should take the form you want it to: a record of your passion for identifying and describing butterflies, an examination of how you spend your time each week with a view to making changes, a consideration of the lack of pattern in your life, a dumping ground for feelings, a place to keep ideas, draft stories, hold a dialogue with an imaginary friend or critic and so on.

If you do not already write a journal or notebook we hope the possibilities mentioned in this section will have whetted your appetite! Over a period of time the way you keep a journal/notebook is likely to change as you discover how to make it a resource that suits you, become a more practised journal writer and as your life itself develops.

Writing an Autobiography

If you have worked your way through many of the exercises in the preceding sections you will have amassed a wealth of autobiographical material which you may wish to develop into a larger whole. This section is about proceeding with this task. It is more concerned with clearing the desk to begin the work than with carrying out the work itself. That, of course, will involve you in a great deal of planning. In an attempt to help you to become clearer about what kind of process you are engaged in, we shall pose questions, and offer some answers, though we would not claim any of them as definitive. All we would suggest is that these are issues of which you should be fully aware before embarking on this enterprise.

Question One: Why Write an Autobiography?

One reason, and probably the most common, is to keep a record for yourself, or for others in your family (especially perhaps your children) of the main outline of your life. We all know individuals, friends or relatives, who led interesting lives or had especially memorable personalities, and we wish that they had written down their experiences. Of course we have no say over the actions of others in this regard, but we *do* exercise control over ourselves and can make the decision to provide an account; it is not an egotistical impulse to wish to write an autobiography, it can be fully justified as a mature resolve, and an attempt, in however small a way, to make a contribution to human knowledge.

It can have even more personal significance than this, though. Writing such an account can form a significant part of an attempt to come to terms with your life, or a part of it, as a mode of self-evaluation. Motivated in this way you will be tracing your life stages and the changes that have taken place in your self in order to gain greater understanding. You are really asking yourself if growth has occurred, whether you have learned anything from what has happened to you. This is a very important process indeed. Joanna Field's *A Life of One's Own* is a book of this kind; she is making discoveries about herself on almost every page.

It may be that before you put pen to paper you are aware that there is a pattern of experience in your life which you already perceive to be something you have in common with others, and which you wish to share, to give them that important sense of identification which can lead to fellow-feeling. Anne Tibble wrote three volumes of autobiography. In the third (*Alone*) she faces life and old age after the death of her husband. What started out as a journal she kept in order to help her to cope, developed into a narrative shaped for an audience.

No-one should imagine that their life is too dull or ordinary to be worth recording. At the least it will have significance for yourself. And if it is presented with honesty and insight it could well be read with interest by others. There are many examples today (Alfred Williams's *To Live It Is To Know It* is one) of life histories by people who have never been in the public eye and would never consider themselves writers, which are vivid and absorbing.

Question Two: Should the Account be Chronological and Continuous?

Most autobiographies do adopt this pattern, and there is no doubt that it is very helpful to you as a writer and as a person to perceive the ups and downs of your life in the order in which things happened to you. It enables you to begin the attempt to evaluate any progress made. You can follow the promptings of your Life-Line (EXERCISE 91 of Self-Portraits and Life-Lines in Part Three) which, if you have also completed EXERCISE 95 of the same section, you will already have expanded into a draft Self-Portrait. Your choice will now be concerned with scale: do you want to expand the whole piece, or concentrate on certain episodes or features?

We are in favour of the widest possible number of approaches. In coming to terms with your life-history (and with the writings which you have already done) you can start anywhere, delve, sift, refine, order, re-order. You are searching for patterns, and it may be that the fractured nature of modern experience is best reflected by a discontinuous narrative.

Perhaps you will wish to focus on a key period in your life, one in which the living was particularly intense, and more changes occurred inside yourself and at a faster rate than at any other time. Brian Keenan's *An Evil Cradling* focuses upon his time as a hostage: the traumatic nature of the experience forced inner development upon him. Maybe in your own case the death of someone close, the break-up of a relationship, an illness or an accident, meeting someone who had a profound influence upon you, or moving away from home to start a new life, provided the trigger for growth and would be an appropriate centrepiece for your account.

For some people it is the outward dramatic events in society, like a war, the growth of a persecution movement, or a devaluation or stock-market crash, which change things irrevocably for them. Eva Hoffman left Poland at the age of 14 to go and live in Canada – hers was a flight from anti-Semitism. It took her well into her adult life to come to terms with the sense of a divided self which resulted from this move, hence the title of her autobiography *Lost in Translation*. The book is divided into three parts: the first deals with her untroubled childhood; the second with the trauma of moving away; the third with the lasting effects of the upheaval.

Autobiographies take many shapes and forms. Some, like Seamus Deane's account of his Derry childhood *Reading in the Dark*, are fact thinly veiled as fiction. John Ward's book *The Wrong Side of Glory* is a personal history in the form of a series of discrete short stories. Eudora Welty in *One Writer's Beginnings* provides the prose equivalent of Wordsworth's poetic approach in *The Prelude*, by concentrating on the early formative period in her life. Louis MacNeice, as well as writing many short poems drawn from his life, essayed two substantial autobiographical narratives. His long poem *Autumn Journal* deals with just a few months in the year 1938; it is like a section cut through the consciousness of an exceptionally intelligent, sensitive individual at a crucial period in his existence. He said that it contained 'rapportage, metaphysics, ethics, lyrical emotion, autobiography, nightmare'. It is also uniquely suffused with the atmosphere of the coming conflict. But it has been said of MacNeice that 'his continuing preoccupation with his own past amounted almost to an obsession' (E R Dodd) and he also wrote a prose account of his life. It covers the whole of his life up to 1939, and then stops, but he did not die until 1963. Another, more eccentric, approach is represented by C H Sisson, whose novel *Christopher Homm* tells of a life with all the events presented backwards. It begins with his subject's death and ends with his birth. This is a fascinating way of tracing the elements that go to form the personality back to their origins, but we are well aware that the reverse chronological approach in its entirety is fortunately not one that is available to ourselves or our readers!

Question Three: Where Does an Autobiography Begin and End?

It is a truism that the story of anyone's life is not the story of one person alone. It would have to include their parents, siblings, partners, children, colleagues and friends if a comprehensive portrait was to be attempted. But should one stop there? Should, for example, the account include an element of family history stretching back generations if that is known? And how can a life not take cognizance of the social and political context in which it was lived out? Fortunately we have provided opportunities in earlier Chapters and Sections for you to begin to take these into account. In deciding on your approach we suggest you list the areas of your life which you consider it essential to include. The work you did on Inner Traits and Outside Influences, Self-Portraits and Life-Lines could prove particularly helpful here.

Edwin Muir offers another interpretation of the parameters of autobiography in his own contribution to the genre, which was originally titled *The Story and the Fable*:

> It is clear that no autobiography can begin with a man's birth, that we extend far beyond any boundary line which we can set for ourselves in the past or the future, and that the life of every man is an endlessly repeated performance of the life of man. It is clear for the same reason that no autobiography can confine itself to conscious life, and that sleep, in which we pass a third of our existence, is a mode of experience, and our dreams a part of reality.

Muir raises an issue of fundamental importance here: how far should the autobiographer attempt to identify shared patterns of experience, those things which lie behind the outward events but which all humans have in common?

And coincidentally, how far should an autobiography be an account of one's dream life as well as waking events? It is significant that both Edwin Muir and Joanna Field use dreams extensively in their writings.

Question Four: What Kind of Balance Should there be Between Narrative and Reflection?

Clearly a life story which restricts itself to a straightforward narrative of outward events is one kind of option, and there are many satisfying books which recreate people, places and happenings with the minimum of reflection and little inclination to reach out for 'significance' (Keith Waterhouse's *There is a Happy Land,* for instance, where a successful attempt is made to get into children's minds, and drawing conclusions from experience would be inappropriate). These, however, require the descriptive and dialogue skills of a novelist.

At the other end of the spectrum are those autobiographies which concentrate upon the nuances of the inner life of the individual. In these a thought or a sensation is an event, to be accorded as much emphasis in the record as winning a prize at school or gaining an Oscar for a film performance. Here is a passage on adolescence from such a book:

> When rage or boredom reappeared, each seemed never to have left. Each so filled me with so many years' intolerable accumulation it jammed the space between my eyes, so I couldn't see. There was no room left even on my surface to live. My rib cage was so taut I couldn't breathe. Every cubic centimetre of atmosphere above my shoulders and head was heaped with last straws. Black hatred clogged my very blood. I couldn't peep, I couldn't wiggle or blink; my blood was too mad to flow.
>
> For as long as I could remember I had been transparent to myself, unselfconscious, learning, doing, most of every day. Now I was in my own way; I myself was a dark object I could not ignore. I couldn't remember how to forget myself, to reckon

myself in, to deal with myself every livelong minute on top of everything else – but swerve as I might, I couldn't avoid it. I was a boulder blocking my own path. I was a dog barking between my own ears, a barking dog who wouldn't hush.

The inventor of these telling metaphors is Annie Dillard from her *An American Childhood*.

Most writers achieve a personal balance between inner and outer which works for them and therefore is likely to be convincing to the reader. Ellen Newton's *This Bed My Centre* records entering a nursing home for the first time as a patient. In the extract we quote in 'Loss' in Part Six she sets out to chronicle her surroundings before withdrawing into the portrayal of her inner feelings.

There is perhaps another kind of reflectiveness involved in some writing, where one is taking the long view, commenting on life generally. John has done a great deal of life history work with older people. Initially he finds that they tend to conceive of the process in terms of list-making – a series of events and people baldly stated without any attempt at evaluation – but after a while the awareness of the approaching end of one's life confers perspective and a sense of philosophical poise (what used to be called 'the wisdom of age'), as in this extract on religious belief by a man in a nursing home who wanted to remain anonymous:

I said to my aunt, 'How do you expect me to be a man at the age of eighteen and believe one person could feed five thousand out of just one loaf and two fishes?' And she said, 'To God all things are possible.' Well, I had no answer to that.

And I saw all the evil in the world and nobody being brought to justice. But she said, 'Laddie, you've got to believe. It doesn't matter whether you're a bad person or not, Jesus will forgive you.' Well, I had no answer to that.

When I speak of any gifts I may have I speak of God. Gifts given to me through my mother. When my mother died, and myself but three days old, she left me motherless, yes, but she left me with more than was taken away.

You will need to experiment with extended pieces of writing until you find the particular balance between telling and commenting with which you feel comfortable.

Question Five: Should the Account be in Prose or Verse?

Autobiographical accounts of a life predominantly use prose, but if your natural medium is poetry there is no reason why you should not attempt to write in that form. The first, and probably still the greatest, poetic autobiography in English is Wordsworth's *The Prelude*, subtitled *The Growth of a Poet's Mind*. In recent times Peter Abbs in his *Icons of Time: An Experiment in Autobiography* has refined his life history to occupy the space of 55 sonnets, which he has grouped in mini-chapters. Many other poets write poems which, although not formally grouped as a sequence, can, when read together, form in the reader's mind (as they probably did in the writer's) a web of interlinked experiences of a profound personal nature. Matt Simpson's book *An Elegy for the Galosherman* is of this kind. All of Sharon Olds' work falls into this category, and the book-length sequence *The Father* unsparingly confronts the central relationship of her life. Donald Atkinson's long poem *A Sleep of Drowned Fathers* also deals with paternal matters; it chronicles the author's formative years in a household in which sexuality and Christianity kept painful company. It is a horrifically convincing meld of circumstantial detail and fevered emotion:

> Indoors she feeds the mangle endless lasagne of washing,
> worries because I'm rising three and haven't talked,
> busy myself instead with dumb flowers, or seek
> identity through injuries. In the sagging
> romper-suit she's knitted me (there was a photograph)
> I climb the bandy pylon legs of the cast-iron mangle,
> feel out its leprosy of blistered green paint.
> My mother on the blind side plunges away with the wheel.

When my fingers minced in the cogs' teeth, the pain
froze in my throat and she went on turning
till I fell to the floor with blood enough to
soak the towel she wrapped my shredded hand in.
Our doctor pudged it back to shape and wondered at my
   dumbness.
But I had more than that to shut my mouth on then.

One of the most striking autobiographical accounts of recent
years is *Heaven's Coast* by Mark Doty. It is described as a
memoir, and is the story of his relationship with his partner
Wally Roberts, who is first of all diagnosed HIV positive
and then dies of AIDS. Many poems in his collections *My
Alexandria* and *Atlantis* share this subject-matter but after
Roberts' death Doty felt the need of the catharsis which
could only be offered by a more extended project. He turned
to prose for the first time and discovered that its inclusiveness
and open-endedness gave him the scope he required:

> to meditate, to describe the experiences of every day and investi-
> gate them for what kind of meaning or metaphor they might
> yield. I think that it would have felt in some way dishonest to
> the gravity and intensity of this time of grief to attempt to order
> it, to shape it in that very controlled way that poems are shaped.
> Potentially, it was an infinite book . . .
>
> *Publishers' World* 15.4.96

The volume has an unusual shape. It begins with what one
might call a series of 'trial-runs', short pieces jumping about
chronologically, each attempting a different angle on a
subject too immediate to get the measure of. Then nearly
half-way into the book Doty is able to settle down to a
straightforward account of what occurred. Even so the narrative takes in quotations from other writers, journal entries,
letters received and written. The Epilogue is an amalgam of
thoughts, anecdotes, jottings. Yet the whole has an aston-
ishing coherence. In one of these end-pieces Doty conveys
valuable insights about what the enterprise achieved for him:

Soon I was impelled, soon I was writing for myself. Writing in a way to save my life, to catch what could be saved of Wally's life, to make form and struggle towards a shape, to make a story of us that can be both kept and given away. The story's my truest possession and I burnish and hammer it and wrestle it to make it whole. In return it offers me back to myself, its embrace and memory larger than mine, more permanent.

Question Six: Should Your Aim be to Tell the Truth and Nothing but the Truth?

Any serious attempt at self-discovery must surely be grounded in the conviction that there are insights buried in your life which are there for the uncovering: 'seek and ye shall find'. Of course the process of discovery may be a painful one, but there is excitement in arrival at the end of a journey, and the new perspectives gained can be helpful in confronting future challenges. We profoundly believe that the knowledge that you have gained in attempting to find out the truth enables you to become more at ease with yourself. Hardy wrote, 'if a way to the Better there be, it exacts a full look at the Worst', but many of the things you will discover about yourself can be reassuring and empowering.

Of course, resolving to seek the truth does not automatically guarantee success in the quest. Indeed it is worth reminding yourself on occasion that the truths uncovered are likely to have more of the relative than the absolute about them. Memory is crucial to your search, and how much is it to be trusted to provide an accurate record of what you thought and felt? As the psychologist F C Bartlett puts it in *Remembering*:

> Remembering appears to be far more decisively an affair of construction rather than of mere reproduction, for as has been shown again and again, condensation, elaboration and invention are common features of ordinary remembering.

So what you are likely to end up with is a hybrid, part-fact part-fiction, in which idealization and avoidance play a part, but where hopefully all the memories and perceptions cohere about a consistent core which we may dare to call 'The Self'. That word 'dare' seems to be an important word in relation to this process. Eudora Welty ends her book with a sentence that could be inscribed above the desk of every autobiographer: 'All serious daring starts from within.'

PART SIX

Themes and Examples

We have suggested a range of techniques to use in exploring yourself and in tackling these you will already have written about people, feelings, problems and concepts that are central to you. In this part we are going to look at some of the main themes we think you will want to explore in depth. We shall quote from writers and comment on their approaches as we think both their subject-matter and methods will give you ideas for tackling your own material. As well as the examples we quote here we shall make other suggestions for further reading.

Early Memories

You often hear people speak of someone as having 'a photographic memory'. By this they mean that the person has the ability to picture places, faces, facts and numbers in detail. There is a strong basis in reality for the existence of this capacity; indeed there is evidence that most of us had it at one time but have lost it. It is scientifically known as *eidetic* which is Greek for 'imaging'.

There have been one or two cases of people who have excelled in this talent throughout their lives, but they have been regarded as freaks and obliged to earn their living on the stage like bearded ladies or the elephant man. Studies have shown, however, that many children possess it – it is perhaps closely allied to Thomas Hood's innocent responses he so much regrets losing (as expressed in his famous poem 'I Remember') – and then they sacrifice it as part of the price of growing up. It is hardly surprising, and not to be blamed on the excessive pressures of our urbanized societies, when you reflect that the child has not learned to discriminate – all sense-impressions are, as it were, grist to his/her mill – whereas the adult must filter out much of what the environment throws at them if they are to make their way in the world.

Whether or not we surround them in a haze of nostalgia, early memories remain among our most vivid, and the literature of childhood, particularly in the twentieth century, is an extensive one. Of course, this chimes in with psychological theories proposing that our earliest experiences are crucial to the development of the mature personality. The Thomas Hood approach would have us believe that childhood is the happiest of times, but as many books have been written to press the claims of the contrary view. Among those we recommend which manage to maintain an optimistic position are *Cider with Rosie* by Laurie Lee and *In the Castle of My Skin* by George Lamming. Lee's book is much the more celebrated of the two; its tranced evocations of a poor rural upbringing in Gloucestershire are laced with humour. Lamming's book is set in Barbados and follows the fortunes of four boys on the beaches and in the village; through their adventures every aspect of change and decay of life in a colonial society is covered, yet nothing is sacrificed in lyrical intensity.

Our extracts have been selected to show differing approaches to childhood. The opening paragraphs of Lamming's book are quoted, a recreation of the young boy being washed by his mother. James Kirkup and Keith Waterhouse both write out of a similar working-class provincial background. Kirkup's approach is meticulously detailed in description (the first volume of his autobiography, from which we quote, only covers the first six years of his life). Here he provides a model of concentrating upon a single object of special significance. If Kirkup's is an exercise in retrospective exactitude, Waterhouse's writing fizzes with energy and humour. It is the sheer high spirits of childhood that he wishes to re-create. Almost every scene in his book (optimistically titled *There is a Happy Land*) is played for laughs. Reading him reminds us how carefree childhood can be, and how ridiculous the world of adults often appears from that vantage-point.

Colin Rowbotham's poem speaks clearly of the way adult relationships can impinge on that youthful *joie de vivre*. He and his brother are aware of a possible disaster they are powerless to comprehend fully, but there is the chance that it may be averted. The passivity of their situation is well symbolized by the game in the gorse-bush.

Caroline Price recalls a childhood game too, in 'Pictures Against Skin', and the sheer ecstasy of the three sisters playing it together in the conspiratorial dark. But this poem includes the adult perspective too – the last verse is full of regrets at the loss of unconditional intimacy which the responsibilities of maturity bring.

Some early memories are distressing and may take years to surface. Frances Angela hints at sexual abuse in her poem 'Strip Wash'.

The extract from *With Both Feet* comes from the autobiography of someone with cerebral palsy. But you do not have to suffer from a physical disability to identify with the plight of Sally O'Shea. We have all at one time or another found ourselves trapped in a situation or place (perhaps school, as here) where we have not chosen to be, and have profoundly wished ourselves elsewhere.

Alfred Williams's solution to this problem, arrived at over a period of time, is to voluntarily exclude himself. His upbringing was in the West Indies, and he tells his story with an unaffected naturalness which gives a lesson to all writers in trusting the speaking voice.

In conclusion, we wish to draw your attention to two pieces by the American Elizabeth Bishop. She was not known for her personal writing, but on this occasion a childhood memory had clearly stuck and demanded expression, and more than once. It occurs at the end of a short story 'The Country Mouse' (to be found in her *Collected Prose*) as well as forming the whole of a poem 'In the Waiting Room'. Bishop was around seven years of age at the time of the incident she is describing and she is waiting while her aunt sees a dentist. In both pieces she experiences a moment of revelation. In the story this is one of personal identity: 'you are *you* and you are going to be *you* forever'. In the poem, which is a much more detailed exploration of the situation, the exact nature of what is being vouchsafed is much less clear: it partakes of her aunt (whose cry comes from the surgery), the other people in the waiting room, even the photographs in the magazine she is reading, as well as the realization of selfhood. It serves as a reminder that experience is a good deal more complex than we sometimes assume, and not easily disentangled in one's mind or formulated in words. It is a reminder, too, that memory is not just eidetic – the passage of time may play tricks on us. Even more potent, perhaps, is the concept that when we write about something that occurred we change it in the act of remembering. So that writing about the same experience on different occasions will result in different interpretations. We suggest it might be helpful to think of memory as a creative force, an active part of the imagination, and as such it becomes one of the most powerful tools in our quest for inner discovery through writing.

From *In the Castle of My Skin*

The skillet was caught up and canted and the water crashed against my head and down my body in a swishing cataract.

'Google google, no more,' I said, 'google google, no more.' The pebbles loosened by moisture from the earth slipped beneath my feet. My arms were thrown out, withdrawn, clasped in a shivering lock, opened again, folded once more. The pebbles shifted under my heels. My body tottered from the rapid, convulsive gasps for breath. Now quiet, erect. Balance perfect. The pebbles re-assorted. The basement firm. I was ready. The hand was hoisted and the skillet poised.

'Yes,' I said, 'I like it so. Slow. Not fast. Just like that.'

The body was firm, hard, erect, a paved brown track down which the water contoured in, out, around, off.

'I want to see,' the voice raised over the neighbouring fence. 'G mother bathing him.'

George Lamming

From *The Only Child*

Another unusual but reassuring sight was Mrs Battey's gas mantle. Its moon-like whiteness was unmarred by any hole or tear. In our street the 'mantle' was almost a sacred object. Ours was always a centre of anguished worry to me since the day when, dancing on the kitchen table, I had touched it with my finger and found it suddenly crumbled away into a fine white dust. Then we had to get a new one, which we could ill afford. How carefully we carried it home in its cardboard carton! When my father had fixed it on the jet and lit it, it flared up alarmingly, and for a time gave no light at all: it was all horribly sooty, and the burning gas inside twinkled desperately inside its little black bag, winking through thousands of tiny holes. Then it slowly turned a deep red, then bright orange, then yellow, then burned to a pure, incandescent whiteness. Whenever I think of Purity, I can't help remembering our gas mantle burning with that hard, fierce light.

James Kirkup

From *There is a Happy Land*

It was better than Christmas, the way we rolled off down the road, shouting and bawling and pretending to limp as though we had cork legs like Mr Bailey. Ted rattled his stick against the railings and chanted: 'Little bit of spice cake, little bit of cheese; glass of cold water, a penny if you please. If you haven't got a penny, halfpenny will do; if you haven't got a halfpenny your door's going through.'

A woman shouted from out of their garden: 'Make a less noise, pair of you! You're like I don't know what!' She was sitting in an armchair near their gate with all her big fat legs showing. There was a big furniture van outside and all carpets in the road and that. They must have been removing. 'Hey, missus, your shirt lap's hanging out!' shouted Ted. We were miles away from where we lived, so nobody could say anything. We started yodelling at her and making burping noises; then we went down the road, walking bow-legged and singing Christmas carols.

Keith Waterhouse

Flowers and Thorns

When Dad and mother went away
To talk out whether they should stay
Together, friends took John and me
Off somewhere for the day.

Was it the summer of the year
That I turned ten? A Saturday
Or Sunday? Strange that details blur
When feelings stay so clear.

Beneath the hot blue day: a heath
Yellow with gorse. Between us both:
Untold anxiety – instead
We played at hide-and-seek

All afternoon. I learned that gorse
Is good to hide inside: the thorns
Won't hurt if they're ignored. Of course
I won the game. I knew

(as kids do) that to win would save
The day somehow. My parents stayed
Together. Gain and loss were too
Entangled to undo.

Colin Rowbotham

Pictures Against Skin

Something in this room. We knew the place
by heart – that never mattered:
sisters following the space from blade
to blade, spiralling round
the nodules of the spine
and up again – a careful phrasing
ended at the full stop of the nape.
Feeling the muscles wriggle, skin
curl up with pleasure
prolonged by guessing wrongly: mirror, vase . . .

They are still here, so many of her things,
the blemished glass, the china

velvety with dust along the sill.
Drawn separately to this room
after the service, we meet
around the massive centrepiece –
not our grandmother's bed, but ours,
thrusting the past insistently
between us. The highlight of each visit:
to sleep all three together, tucked

beneath the perfumed camouflage
of eiderdowns, sliding down,
our spirits soon subsiding
into hushed intent – the games devised
to bridge the chasm yawning
before sleep.
Fingers delicately drawing in the dark
translated into pictures passed
from back to back
our speechless happiness at being here.

I have let slip the memory, and laugh;
and wonder, too,
which of us is ever touched in that way
now, with such tenderness.
And in a rare apologetic movement
we lean across the faded quilt,
lips grazing lips, a cheek, searching beneath
the scent we choose to wear to funerals
a trace of that familiarity,
the odour of another, younger skin.

Caroline Price

Strip Wash

I'm standing half-covered
in a vest
in a round bowl
in the kitchen sink;
one hand reaching out
to steady myself
on the window-glass.

I can see the bottom
of the narrow stairs;
the clothes-line
pullied to the ceiling,
my father's overall straps
with the twinkling, silver buckles
hanging down.
And the top of my mother's dark head
as I struggle to balance
spreading my legs for her fingers
beneath the flannel.

Frances Angela

From *With Both Feet*

My brother John drove the car up the steep winding driveway
and came to a halt outside the double-fronted doors of the
building. I was seven years old and felt tension that something
was about to happen which had not been explained to me. Dad
said nothing and remained in the car. Mum, cradling me in her
arms, walked through the doors into the silent, stuffy atmosphere
of the building which smelt of strangeness. John followed with
my case.

A big woman with plaits wound around the top of her head,
a pale face, small steely blue eyes and fat bulbous cheeks, came
and introduced herself as Mrs Collier. She was wearing a white
overall and said she was to be my housemother. As I felt her
powerful hands reaching out and taking me from my mother,
panic struck and my limbs leapt into uncontrolled action. My
arms flailed out as my face was smothered in her huge, hard
bosom and my long straggly hair caught on one of her buttons,
making me wince with pain. Waves of confusion and terror
coursed through my stomach and travelled up to my throat
making me feel as if I was bursting.

Hot tears sprang to my eyes and trickled their saltiness down
into the corners of my mouth, as, struggling to turn my head, I
managed to glimpse for just a few seconds, the figures of two
people I loved and trusted retreating out of the school doors
leaving me in this alien woman's arms. Suddenly a quick, invol-
untary spasm chucked my face back into her bosom, where I

did not want it to rest. I longed desperately to rid myself of her loathsome body and somehow fly after my mother and brother out into the car, to be driven back home to safety and security.

'All right, Sal, listen, listen,' she repeated over and over again as she carried me down a long, dimly-lit corridor. All I could see were hazy flashes of light and a misty white ceiling through my water-filled eyes. My exhausted body was clammy and empty and my throat ached as my crying continued. I felt myself being laid on a hard, wooden-slatted board fitted over a bath. Intruding fingers undressed me. Every now and again my elbows or fingers got caught or entangled between the unfamiliar slats and had to be prised out. The bathroom echoed Mrs Collier's words making them seem louder so that I cried even harder. She carried my crushed, sobbing body to a dark room with three small hospital-style beds along each wall, placed me between ice-cold sheets, tucked me in tightly and left me.

Her voice trailed off into the distance still saying 'All right, Sal, listen, listen.' What I was supposed to listen to I did not know or care about. All I wanted was to be at home and I vowed I would be good for evermore if I got there.

Sally O'Shea

From *To Live It is to Know It*

Every day you had to know your lesson, what people here call 'homework'. You do this little lesson at home and take it into school on the next day. Well I didn't get no time for this homework, all my time were taken up looking after my father horse and goat and so on. And when I finish my day, which start at five or six in the morning and don't finish till seven or eight at night, I did not think about homework, I did think about some play. I were only seven so I had to go out and do a bit of playing.

So, next morning, after doing my work with father animals, I in school and I have not done my homework. Then I get the cane. And I *did* get cane. Many time. And I do not mean sugar cane, I mean beating on the hand so they bruise and hurt. The answer seem to me to be . . . don't go to school.

After that, most of the time I just didn't go. As I get near the school I see the teacher drilling the kids in the yard, making them march. I look at them, and think how Mr Simms will cane me, and I walk past and turn into the first field I find. But I can't go too far from school, because I had to go home for my dinner at twelve o'clock. The only way I could know what's going on, and be home so mother don't know I'm not at school, is to watch the school from the tallest tree around. That's why I say I spend most of my schooldays up a tree!

About ten to twelve each day the kids in school did sing a song, and that let me know that it time to go home for dinner and I say to myself, 'All right, they singing a song, it about time I come down out of this tree.'

Alfred Williams (with Ray Brown)

Life Stages

It is always illuminating to examine the maps of our lives, compare past with present, trace the routes by which we reached the selves we are today. In this section we are looking at writing which captures or reflects on particular stages in individual lives.

We started this part of the book with the theme of childhood, so here we are beginning with puberty, that difficult and intense period when one is neither adult nor child. Laurie Lee catches the essence of that time wonderfully in *Cider with Rosie* when he re-creates the afternoon on which Rosie lured him away from the haymaking and took him under the hay wagon. The writing, both lively and sensual, encapsulates sexual awakening, its excitement and fear, its clumsiness and preciousness. It also suggests the dreamy heat of fields which surrounds the memory of the event.

D H Lawrence's novel *Sons and Lovers*, has a strong autobiographical basis. It traces the intense and complex passions of the young man who is its main character. Growing up also means fending for oneself. Some people begin by treating adult life as an adventure and set off on travels as the young Laurie Lee did to Spain. He wrote about this period of his life in the second volume of his autobiography: *As I Walked Out One Midsummer Morning*.

Others find themselves discovering much about life when they start work. John Ward, whose first job was in a poor area of Liverpool, drew directly on this experience in some of his short stories. The piece we quote shows how exact and detailed his recall is of people, place and feeling.

Working in factories, unemployment, considering the nature of work – these are not often topics for poems but they are central themes to American poet Philip Levine. Our extract from a poem called 'Fear and Fame' is graphically written and makes it easy for the reader to follow the technical operation described. The poet uses rich language with a wide range of reference and an expansive but sinewy free verse form. We learn more or less incidentally how much at ease he is with his workmates.

Ursula Fanthorpe left a safe career in teaching to work as a medical clerk. She has written several ironic and compassionate poems about the world of hospital. In *Testament of Youth* Vera Brittain wrote about her initiation into nursing during World War One and described in detail the experience of nursing seriously wounded soldiers in France.

Sadly, even now, being a soldier continues to be a stage in life in certain parts of the world and some do not survive it. The horror of war has been recorded by well-known and little-known writers. Wilfred Owen has described the day-to-day misery of war and questioned its futility both in his poems and his letters to his mother, Susan Owen.

Partnership/marriage marks a new stage in life, one often viewed romantically but not in Jonathan Davidson's jokey poem 'Now We Are Married', which takes a look at sharing and demarcation lines. 'Eve of Removal' by Caroline Price is a look at a three-year marriage. The moving out of a two-roomed flat highlights how unsettled the writer feels and the poem anticipates separation.

Entering the stage of parenthood is dramatic and because we mostly live in smaller units now new mothers often have little family support and know nothing about babies.

Becoming a mother, therefore, can be difficult especially as the idea of motherhood is so often idealized. In her direct and honest book *The Mother Knot*, Jane Lazerre, a Jewish woman married to a black man, examines her own experiences and emotions. We quote an extract which shows how she fuelled her sense of inadequacy by comparing herself with another mother.

A number of women become parents without a partner. Others suffer because they cannot have a child. (See Loss further on in Part Six where we describe Jacqueline Brown's *Thinking Egg* which treats this subject in depth.) Many people do not settle into long-term partnerships but nevertheless develop their lives. New Zealand writer Janet Frame did this after spending eight harrowing years in mental hospitals, wrongly diagnosed as schizophrenic. In the last part of her second volume of autobiography, *An Angel at My Table*, she relates how she found confidence with the help of another writer, Frank Sargeson, who let her live in his garden shed. Then in *An Envoy from Mirror City*, the third volume, she relates how she travelled to Europe where she lived in near-poverty in London, Ibiza and Andorra where she made new friends, had some formative short-term relationships and found herself both as a person and a writer.

Mid-life is often a period of re-assessment or realization, a time when there is a searching for a different kind of fulfilment. It was at this stage that Ursula Fanthorpe left teaching to do low-grade work in a hospital. Mimi Khalvati responds to this period of life in the poem 'Reaching the Midway Mark', which is a series of imaginative impressions, each setting off the next as a question.

Middle-aged people often find they have to take responsibility for their frail parents and in her tender poem 'Bathing My Mother', Frances Wilson shows how her mother has now become her child. Her mother's behaviour reminds the poet of her daughter as a toddler and then that she, herself, has now passed childbearing age.

In Part Five: Keeping a Journal, we referred to the diary Anne Tibble kept as a way of talking to her husband after his death. The entries report on her life as well as looking at herself with an honesty which is sometimes scathing.

We end this section with 'A Clear Shell' by Frances Bellerby. In this visionary and spiritual poem about the experience of extreme pain, the strict rhymed form contrasts with the boundlessness of the pain. The poem ends by welcoming death.

From *Cider with Rosie*

We crawled underneath, between the wheels, into a herb-scented cave of darkness. Rosie scratched about, turned over a sack, and revealed a stone jar of cider.

'It's cider,' she said. 'You ain't to drink it though. Not much of it, any rate.'

Huge and squat, the jar lay on the grass like an un-exploded bomb. We lifted it up, unscrewed the stopper, and smelt the whiff of fermented apples. I held the jar to my mouth and rolled my eyes sideways, like a beast at a waterhole [. . .]

Never to be forgotten, that first long secret drink of golden fire, juice of those valleys and of that time . . . Never to be forgotten, or ever tasted again [. . .]

[. . .] I turned to look at Rosie. She was yellow and dusty with buttercups and seemed to be purring in the gloom; her hair was rich as a wild bee's nest and her eyes were full of stings. I did not know what to do about her, nor did I know what not to do. She looked smooth and precious, a thing of unplumbable mysteries, and perilous as quicksand.

Laurie Lee

From *Shoes*

When I left school I went to work among the inhabitants of the north end of Liverpool. I had nothing in common with them. They were Irish, Catholic, and so antagonistic to civil authority that the police went about in pairs, even in daylight . . . I was English, prim, inclined to be anti-clerical, and worst of all an official [. . .]

I had to visit this house [. . . it] stood in a court of eight identical houses [. . .] the window at street level was broken and patched with a big sheet of cardboard. A child squatted on the doorstep [. . .] Her hair was hanging in long rats' tails, her dark eyes were shuttered, and her little monkey's face, smeared with dirt, was blank as a poker player's. What a place, I told myself, what a simply *bloody* place [. . .]

A woman was walking towards me. She wore a black woollen shawl over her head and shoulders and she shuffled along slowly in down-at-heel shoes [. . .] She walked leaning backwards slightly, carrying her huge belly in front of her like a drum.

The child scrambled to her feet [. . .] When she was a few feet away, she opened her arms and threw herself upon her mother. Her face seemed to glow. You could see her again as she must have been before marriage and children and poverty had eroded her strength and good looks [. . .] my irritation seemed suddenly petty and shameful. I was humbled by the smile and the child's spontaneous incandescence on seeing her mother.

John Ward

From 'Fear and Fame'

Half an hour to dress, wide rubber hip boots,
gauntlets to the elbow, a plastic helmet
like a knight's but with a little glass window
that kept steaming over, and a respirator
to save my smoke-stained lungs. I would descend
step by slow step into the dim world
of the pickling tank and there prepare
the new solutions from the great carboys
of acids lowered to me on ropes – all from a recipe
I shared with nobody and learned from Frank O'Mera
before he went off to the bars on Vernor Highway
to drink himself to death. A gallon of hydrochloric
steaming from the wide glass mouth, a dash
of pale nitric to bubble up, sulphuric to calm,
metals for sweeteners, cleansers for salts,
until I knew the burning stew was done.
Then to climb back, step by stately step, the adventurer
returned to the ordinary blinking lights

of the swingshift at Feinberg and Breslin's
First-Rate Plumbing and Plating with a message
from the kingdom of fire. Oddly enough
no one welcomed me back, and I'd stand
fully armoured as the downpour of cold water
rained down on me and the smoking traces puddled
at my feet like so much milk and melting snow.
Then to disrobe down to my work pants and shirt,
my black street shoes and white cotton socks,
to reassume my nickname, strap on my Bulova,
screw back my wedding ring, and with tap water
gargle away the bitterness as best I could.

Philip Levine

Now We Are Married

You've polished the cut glass vase
and the two rose bowls. I'm ironing
because if I've cooked I will not
wash-up, unless you have vacuumed,
which you'll only do if the yard
has been swept within the last week.
When I either remove or rebuild
the ex-post office bicycle
under the stairs you'll consider
filing your correspondence. Today
I'd thought of grouting tiles. I didn't
because I understood the bathroom
was within your jurisdiction,
in which case I would happily
take charge of the study – if we had
a study. As it is I'd agreed
to see to the decorative glassware.
I do the decorative glassware.
So tell me, *why* have you polished
the two rose bowls and the cut glass vase?

Jonathan Davidson

Eve of Removal

It is past midnight; we are trying to sleep
humped under the last sheet,
curled in the shadow of tea-chests stacked

high as apartment blocks.
All our worldly good in those. Denuded,
the windows stare out for newcomers,

the telephone waits. Lined up,
the last slippers, last pair of shoes,
the last case gaping, left undone for toothbrushes.

The trains disturb me for the first time
since my first night here, three years ago.
Three years! in these two rooms,

from our quiet wedding through even quieter times
to this, not needing any more to talk
or touch toes for comfort in the bed:

I never really did unpack my things here,
never really settled, and therefore feel no twinge.
Two cats fight outside, sporadically.

I make resolutions. This time I'll try.
It will be different: a home, with room
for family to stay, a garden, cupboard space;

we'll be all right. A proper house. You say
that I will never rest, must uproot constantly.
With fingers crossed I feel an old defiance.

This time home. Our home. I vow I'll stay.
I stretch across to touch you, but not quite.
Two cats fight outside, then move away.

Caroline Price

From *The Mother Knot*

Was she lying? I wondered, this young, innocent, white and pink
midwestern girl who had a good baby. Was her baby really as
bad as mine, did he cry all night and nurse every hour instead

of every four, and stay constipated for two or three days at a time, or was he really the way she declared him to be? I looked closely at her eyes, stared for so long I made her uncomfortable, waited in ambush to spot a sign of hypocrisy in a line of her face, a twist of her mouth. But always she appeared to be even, serene, impenetrable. Once I listened at her baby's window for screams in the night. I heard none. I began to hate her and her baby.

Jane Lazerre

Reaching the Midway Mark

reaching, for some reason, out for it
only to wake in a darkened room
where chair and clothes and bed

have no more weight than air has
in daytime when all these things
are solid . . . mother, tell me.

Poet-mother, born of another
generation speaking through its own
veil, have you told me? I cannot find it.
Not the marrow, not the heart of it.
Is it

like daring to fill a room with light
when the house is dark . . .

how silence thins . . .
how sounds rush through in a sudden flood
but nothing breaks, not one thin strand
of silk? Is it

like prising open a fruit to find
torn ligatures of strawberry? Blue,

a blue that goes with Egyptian gold,
the bluest of blues the minute before
night thins itself with morning? Heavy,

disembodied? How the first time feels
when you ask a man *can I kiss you*, is it

how day and night change places?
To do with articles of clothing?
All the things I could tell you mother?
All the things they tell me.

Mimi Khálvati

Bathing My Mother

You hang back, call me
cruel, assure me you'll fall,
promise impossible behaviour,
anything to avoid that one step
into the treachery of white.

Years ago my baby daughter
would list implausible excuses –
a wobbly tooth, a hurting finger,
because her teddy said so –
to escape the ordeal of water.

Once in, of course, you're soothed,
though you won't admit it, fiddle
with bubbles while I soap your skin –
so thin, but soft as a child's –
fumble into intimacies,

glad of steamed-up glasses.
Wrapped in a warm towel, later,
you punish me with stiff
resistance, as I pat talc
into your shrunk hollows,

my belly tight, braced against
your slight weight, your need,
your terror, my fury, a longing
which takes my breath away
for another baby I'll never bear.

Frances Wilson

From *Alone*

Waking about half-past five this morning, I watch the waning
moon overtake the morning star, the sun about to rise below

them. As in a flash I see *through* the fear, renunciation and toil
I have had for my dwelling place. I might even face death free
of fear. A small revelation, due, perhaps, to meeting the vastness
just now beside my own insignificance, makes me calmer than I
have been since you left.

Of course pain is still to be reckoned with. Should I try to
escape that? If one lives carefully enough – or carelessly – eats
simple food, drinks little or no alcohol, does not pamper one's
body or over-indulge its avidnesses, or be idle, can one escape
disease and pain? I'll tell you later.

Anne Tibble

A Clear Shell

Then fire burned my body to a clear shell.
Though whether the fanning tempest blew from hell
Or heaven I could not, cannot, tell –
Who have no sense
Left for so nice a difference.

But I learned the essential function of extreme pain –
Of liquid fire pouring again and again
And again through the horrified body: such pain
Makes wholly innocent.
Therefore am I impenitent

Today. Today ask no forgiveness,
Having nothing to be forgiven. And my soul, no less
House-proud than at the beginning, shows Death
Smilingly over the place,
Trusting this new face.

Frances Bellerby

Relationships

We have already suggested some approaches to use in exploring relationships (in particular in Part Three: Relationships, Families and Other Groups.) In this section we are going to look at some ways in which writers have tackled this central theme.

We begin with an extract from *I Know Why The Caged Bird Sings*, the first volume of Maya Angelou's autobiography. It shows the writer's strong, unquestioning love as a child for her brother. She describes how she sees him in contrast to herself and then relates a humorous incident which illustrates how he protects her.

In his powerful autobiography, *An Evil Cradling*, Brian Keenan traces his journey of self-discovery during the years he was imprisoned as a hostage in Beirut. Important in this process was the growth of a close friendship between himself and John McCarthy, another hostage, with whom he shared a cell for much of the time he was shut away. Brian Keenan analyses this relationship, showing the enormous strength it gave both of them in coping with a long imprisonment. Our extract is a description of an early stage in the friendship.

In 'Alders' closeness is shown obliquely. On the surface the tone is light, conversational. Direct address is used and the poem is set round an everyday action – hanging and re-hanging a picture. But in drawing a parallel with the alders Hubert Moore lets through feelings of tenderness, and the intensity of love for a partner suddenly surfaces with the exclamation 'Love, startlingly upright'.

Liz Houghton also focuses on an action in 'Caustic Soda'. Here the scrubbing equates with the strength of feeling. The poem shows not only the nature of the love she and her father share but her new understanding – because her baby has just died – of the tie between child and parent.

In her poem 'Keeping in Touch' Jan Jenkins uses humour to underline the feelings which surface when her daughter leaves home. The reader, taken into the writer's train of thought, identifies with her. The apt kite image is a reminder of the emotional umbilical cord between mother and child.

William Ayot gives us a glimpse of a destructive relationship in 'Never', a poem in which he states his anger with his father and the guilt he is left with after his father's death. 'Odi et Amo' by Irene Rawnsley is an expression of hatred in a dramatic extended metaphor. It shows how a failed marriage has damaged her. The tight lyrical form of the poem counterpoints its mood.

In some relationships the strongest element is their tenuousness and this is uppermost for Brian Jones as he describes with unsparing honesty the predicament of the children of broken marriages. He notes how separate he is from his own children, how cut off they must feel and therefore how easy communication is impossible.

Often a writer's main concern in presenting a central relationship is to show a whole complex of feelings, which may be ambivalent and changing. Susan Wicks began writing about her father to help herself cope with him after her mother died. Then she developed her notebook entries into a book, *Driving My Father*. This explores her relationship with both parents in a series of cameos which include the present and its day-to-day practicalities, memories, dreams and projections. The two brief extracts we include show something of the range of her feelings about her father.

Scar Tissue, a searching novel by Michael Ignatieff, is based on personal experience. The main character examines his relationship with his mother, brother, wife and himself as the illness of dementia gradually destroys his mother. (See the extract in Loss in the next section.)

In *Honeymoon* Caroline Price draws on outer detail and recalls inner feelings to convey the charge and atmosphere at a particular point in a relationship, also to note the beginnings of changes in it. Before starting on this autobiographical chapter, she spent days re-living the period it related to until she felt ready to re-create it in writing. The piece is one of a series she has produced partly to explore herself and partly as preparation for a work of fiction.

Destructive and supportive relationships, their complexities, ambivalences and nuances – this is the subject-matter of poet Sharon Olds. She writes in close-up with a frankness which can be dramatic or poignant about her relationships with her parents, partner and children. We recommend the poem 'My Son The Man' for the subtle thought behind the striking *trunk* image. It is in her collection *The Wellspring* which is a good starting point for readers who do not know Sharon Olds' work.

From *I Know Why the Caged Bird Sings*

Bailey was the greatest person in my world. And the fact that he was my brother . . . was such good fortune that it made me want to live a Christian life just to show God that I was grateful. Where I was big, elbowy and grating, he was small, graceful and smooth. When I was described by our playmates as being shit colour, he was lauded for his velvet-black skin [. . .] And yet he loved me.

When our elders said unkind things about my features (my family was handsome to a point of pain for me), Bailey would wink at me from across the room, and I knew that it was a matter of time before he would take revenge. He would allow the old ladies to finish wondering how on earth I came about, then he would ask, in a voice like cooling bacon grease, 'Oh Mizeriz Coleman, how is your son? I saw him the other day, and he looked sick enough to die.'

Aghast, the ladies would ask, 'Die? From what? He ain't sick.'

And in a voice oilier than the one before, he'd answer with a straight face, 'From the Uglies.'

Maya Angelou

From *An Evil Cradling*

The size of the room allowed us sufficient space to exercise. We would walk around it in single file and often in silence try to measure out the miles we could walk in a day. For the sheer hell of it we would argue about who had walked furthest in the past week . . . Neither of us sought to outdo or diminish the other but simply to set a challenge for ourselves [. . .] We would talk into the small hours as we fantasized our bottle of water to be a very strong red wine. Our imagination had performed a Cana-like miracle. We babbled drunkenly.

Our life histories were no longer exclusive preserves. For as we told our different stories of friends and of families we exchanged each other's friends and families until they became our own. People we had never met became vividly real to us. We began to move into each other's lives.

Brian Keenan

Alders

One of the alders stands exactly like you,
or rather two of them do.

No one could say that you loll or prop
your weight on a hip,

yet when you draw yourself up to take
that long critical look

at something I've done – cut a tree down,
re-hung a picture – one

of your legs (your left, my right) falters
loose at the knee, while the other's

the perfect alder, tapering, straight.
Love, startlingly upright

you who mean what you say
and say I should re-hang inches away

from where I've already re-hung,
and believe in something

balanced and final and good, inching
upwards towards it, branching

and branching – love, one of the alders
(your left, my right) falters.

Hubert Moore

Caustic Soda

The week the first baby died
my father visited –
awkward and lost in the new house
with stains on the floor
that would not fade.

While I was crying in hospital
he was on his knees,
not praying – scrubbing
with caustic soda and wire wool –
heedless for hours
with no gloves on.

He hid his red and bleeding hands –
said he hadn't felt the pain.
I held them gently, scolding,
not needing to say
that I'd learned how it feels
to love your child that way.

Liz Houghton

Keeping in Touch

At last, long distance
her voice, lately of the breakfast table
but now three hundred miles away.
A young and tender landscape
of a voice, the up and down of it
drawing me through unfamiliar pathways.
Is she all right?
This and other questions
press against the lump
which is my throat.

Exalted by the telling
of her news and a life airborne
by fresh excitements, she flies now
like a kite cajoled by the distance
between us and the wistful tug,
tug of my affirmatives.
Dearest daughter, I will write
every week if necessary
and will you phone

now and again?

Jan Jenkins

Never

The night my father died
he hit me.
In an extremity of pain

or whisky-rage or both,
one arm dead already,
he lashed out with the other

to send me spinning across
the floor, more shamed,
more shocked than truly hurt.

I took my tears and hid them,
nursed them
till I heard him on the stairs.

I'm sorry I hit you, he said
and I waited.
Let's make it up, old son.

Never – I spat out years
of resentment.
Never – and I turned away.

He left me then, and later
when I found him
the word was in the air.

Never – the dead forget
but a single word
can ride the living for life.

William Ayot

Odi et Amo

I wanted you
like lion skin
      to wrap
           my coward courage in.

I wanted you
to make it grow;
      you fed it poison
         sweet and slow.

Into each dream
the hemlock spread
      to feed a monster
        in my head.

Now every night
my fingers try
      to stop its breath
     but it won't die.

Irene Rawnsley

The Children of Separation

While waiting for you to come, I imagine you sitting
in a stopped train between stations, feeling
at peace in no-man's land, where there is no need
to say 'we' or 'our' or 'home', or other impossible words,

where the poppies among the corn
recall distant universal pain
cushioned in history and innocence.
How unusual it must be for you now to enjoy silence,

with no-one to crave your assurance, no-one to grasp
your hands, stare into your face, and guiltily ask
'Are you all right? Are you unhappy? Will you say?'
No-one you must gratify

with tears, or the absence of tears.
Suddenly, you are among the ranks of those
who once seemed as unlikely, as remote,
as the handicapped, the poor, the mad –

the children of separation, those who are given
two Christmases to halve the pain
and find it doubled, those who are more prey
to nostalgia than old men, who have been betrayed

by language and now handle it like bombs,
for whom affection is a thicket of spies, and surnames
amputations with the ache of wholeness.
Every book taken down is inscribed by loving parents,

and albums of photographs refuse to be otherwise.
What can be done with memories?
What remains of the self if everything that was
is now framed in the inverted commas of 'seemed'?

I imagine the brakes sighing to the inevitable,
and the train resuming the purpose of the rails.
Soon you will step out into my story
whose pages for too long I kept closed to you.

We will walk through fields I am still making mine,
and when the time comes for someone to say 'Let's go home'
no-one will say it. On the platform, we will wait to be parted,
your hand clutching a ticket to somewhere rejected.

Brian Jones

From *Driving My Father*

Everything my father ever made was special. When I was small
my parents rented an upstairs flat in a big old Victorian house
on the edge of a village. But we had the use of a garden. In the
garden my father built me a swing [. . .]

It was a permanent fixture of that first garden. I was in tears
as we drove away. But my father could do anything. When the
removal lorry drew up at the new house, I screamed with delight.
There was the swing, perched on top of our pile of tea-chests
and shabby furniture. My father was grinning at me. The creo-
soted legs stuck out from the heap, still encased in their concrete
boots [. . .]

* * *

One day I shall be looking in the larder for a can of beans.
'They're not in there,' my father will say. 'We don't keep them
in there.'

'Where do you keep them?' I shall ask him.

He will look at me as if I am a half-wit. 'In the garage. In the
meat-safe. With the evaporated milk and the sardines.'

I won't sigh. 'I'd better go out there and get them.' But he
won't let me [. . .]

And I shall be left looking into the open pantry, at the old
chipped enamel saucepans, the row of hot-water bottles upside
down on their hooks, the extra spin-drier they kept for emerg-
encies, an old handbag of mine full of clothes-pegs. And next to
it a big white plastic carrier-bag, bulging. I shall reach into it.

When he comes back he will put the tin of beans down on the
stained yellow counter. He will reach into the drawer for a tin-
opener. He will grunt as he presses the metal tooth down into
the lid. The steel butterfly will begin to turn shakily on its axis.

Then, from behind him, I shall raise my arms like a dancer
and bring the plastic bag down smoothly over his head.

Susan Wicks

From *Honeymoon*

I will him to turn and take a photo of me leaning back into
spray, my hair tangled and streaming. I am the woman he used
to watch, whose face he imagined for years beneath him, above
him, superimposed on other faces. How has he learnt so quickly
to take me in his stride? I am so happy, he says again. I feel I
could have anything I want [. . .] Confidence frightens me; I want
him to shake, to tremble, like he used to. I put my hands over
his and stare up into his face. His eyes are deeply on me; he
smiles: What is it? The corners of his mouth curl as he waits.
And in the silence I suddenly understand that what he and I
want is the same, will always be the same; and I turn my head
away, bewildered and somehow ashamed to have found this out.
But I am so strong – holding him in my arms after we have
made love, after he has reared from my body with that strange
cry of his, arching his back for a moment and then falling straight
into sleep; I am strong – because I can't fall too, I won't; even
in this room which, home to our longest time together, has
become special, completely ours.

Caroline Price

LOSS

The limited span of life, its unpredictability, the shortcomings in human behaviour mean that we all experience loss and deprivation in various forms which affect us profoundly. Because we have the ability to hope and think ahead loss often means the disappointment of an expectation.

The most final form of loss is bereavement. When someone close dies: a parent, partner, child, lover or friend, many people feel the need to express their feelings in a poem, a letter or other piece of writing whether they think of themselves as writers or not. As well as being a way of keeping the person it is a tangible expression of grief, part of the process of coming to terms with the loss.

We begin by recommending Douglas Dunn's *Elegies*. The poems in this book are about his wife, Lesley – their life together, her illness, death and the stages of grief he went through. They are direct, tender and laden with a sense of emptiness.

In 'Widowhood' Phoebe Hesketh uses nature imagery to express the bleakness she still feels 13 years after the death of her husband. In contrast in 'Four Years' Pamela Gillilan conveys loss by recording in exact, unadorned detail how all evidence of her husband in the house has gone, how she hangs onto the hope that it still contains some vestige of him. We recommend this and other poems about her loss in her book *All Steel Traveller.*

The extract from *Scar Tissue*, Michael Ignatieff's novel based on personal experience, pinpoints the moment when the main character realizes he has lost his mother because dementia has destroyed her powers of recognition. The description concentrates on her eyes, comparing them with the lights of a sinking ship. The repeated reference to the unseeing eyes brings home the sense of shock.

The failure of a relationship to offer what is longed for is a major form of loss for many people. It is the subject of Irene Rawnsley's 'Odi et Amo' (*see* Part Six: Relationships). The poem describes in metaphor the terrible consequence of her partner's failure to nurture her.

In her short sequence, 'Mother', Isobel Thrilling writes starkly about how and why her mother deprived her of love. We include the second poem which describes in metaphor the distance and enmity between mother and daughter. It ends with the sense of destitution which the poet still feels. We also include the third poem. This is built round an extended image which shows how the writer was treated as a child. It is also a marvellous example of how much can be conveyed in highly charged, compressed writing. This sequence is in *Spectrum Shift* which has a number of poems about grief and different kinds of loss.

Pascale Petit has explored her broken childhood and loss of parenting in poems which are also descriptions of real and metaphorical journeys to distant landscapes. Our extract is from 'Icefall Climbing in Tibet'. Brian Jones also writes about a broken family in 'Children of Separation' (*see* Part Six: Relationships). In this poem he details losses felt both by the children and also himself, their father.

The central theme of Jacqueline Brown's book-length poem sequence, *Thinking Egg*, is childlessness. The poems follow the writer through her life: childhood, puberty, her mother's death, first love, marriage, the stages of a breakdown when she finds out she's infertile and how she comes to terms with her situation. Jane Duran treats childlessness very differently. In her poem 'Forty Eight', she fantasizes that she is pregnant and with images of town and sea fabricates a daydream she is reluctant to relinquish.

Disablement is another kind of loss. In her autobiography Helen Keller, who was left blind and deaf by illness as a very small child, describes how she experienced this and her gradual and extraordinary emergence as she learnt to communicate. When Molly Holden developed an illness that paralysed her she began to write poetry. Close observation of her surroundings and intense memories are features of her work. Her poem 'Upstairs Light' records intimate details of the upstairs world which has a new significance for her now she can no longer visit it.

It is not unusual for loss to lead to new insights, compensations. Ellen Newton, an Australian writer and broadcaster in her seventies, lost her freedom when she agreed to live in a nursing home because she was suffering from angina. In despair at her incarceration she began to write a diary. Doing this helped her to endure her situation and after a few years she decided to turn her entries into a book. The achievement gave her the courage to reject nursing-home life and live independently again. Here is a graphic example of how writing can change one's life. In the paragraph we quote the contrast between her descriptions of the home and her references to life outside emphasizes her sense of being trapped.

Sufferers from mental illness usually feel imprisoned inside themselves and those who spend a period of time in a mental hospital often find this an incarceration too. In *Faces in the Water*, a novel based on her own experiences, Janet Frame (whose autobiographies we referred to in Part Six: Life Stages) re-creates in detail the horror of being mis-diagnosed and shut away in an institution. The piece included here shows how the main character's behaviour was dictated by the way the hospital staff treated her, how much she felt at their mercy.

We have already included an extract from Brian Keenan's *An Evil Cradling* in Part Six: Relationships. This powerful autobiography encompasses the years he was imprisoned as a hostage in Beirut. It traces how he climbed out of the despair of the inner world he had retreated to during months of solitary confinement, how he found himself although he'd lost his physical freedom.

A different kind of loss – but one that is not at all uncommon now so many people move away from the country where they spent their early childhood – is the loss of language, relatives, familiar foods, customs, a whole culture. Eva Hoffman left Poland in 1939 at the age of thirteen to go and live in Vancouver. In her perceptive book *Lost in Translation*, she examines the stages she had to go through to come to terms with the duality of her life. Our piece shows an immediate result of the uprooting was the deprivation of an inner language.

We end this section by recommending two poems which look at the nature of loss. In 'One Art', Elizabeth Bishop says one must practise losing possessions in order to 'master the art of losing'. This famous poem, which is both personal and impersonal, lists increasingly greater losses: houses, cities, continents, a much loved person. The strict villanelle form and the ironic tone counterpoint the immensity of loss we all suffer as human beings. 'The Ball Poem' by James Berryman begins with a description of a child's devastation because he has lost his ball in the water. The ball becomes a metaphor as the poet considers the understanding of loss everyone must learn.

Widowhood

After thirteen years
nothing is changed except
the years like birds

have printed my face with their feet
and my side of the bed
is hollow.
I've tunnelled a path from myself
to the world
but summer weeds choke it, and snow,
and my warm-handled shovel is thin
as the song of an autumn robin.

Phoebe Hesketh

From *Scar Tissue*

Then an evening came, like thousands before it, when I entered her room and she was lying in bed, with her hands upon the covers, her ancient face lit by the bedside lamp, and she turned slowly at the sound of my footsteps and looked at me. I stood still and her gaze continued, clear, focused and entirely indifferent. Then she looked away ... I remembered the night I had been on the hillside and how the farm in the distance had looked like the Andrea Doria, that ship going down through the ocean, with its lights left on, blazing through the dark. The eyes that do not see ... I had arrived at the moment, long foretold, hopelessly prepared for, when Mother took the step beyond her self and moved into the world of death with her eyes open.

Michael Ignatieff

From 'Mother'

2.
Silences
between us like
black owls asleep,

we smile
across quiet talons,
feather on feather
trapping soft darkness.

Images of blood
and tearing
make us fear to wake

these birds
that eat our light.

They hunt in dreams.

If I could speak,
I would ask
why there is always a child
crying in my head.

I remember my father's
whip of words,
but you are nebulous,
bright but insubstantial:

I needed you solid as bread.

3.
My mother took
my skin
to wrap my sister in,

I grew
another that was new
and very thin:

she gave that too.

Isobel Thrilling

From 'Icefall Climbing in Tibet'

I am facing the icefall at the base of Everest.
A great white city is slowly subsiding.
The walls are never the same, never quiet.
An avalanche lands with a suppressed sigh.
I put on my crampons, sharpen my axe,
pass through the gate, which collapses after me.
Some of the rooms have crumbled. Some are lit
by the blue and pink lamps of my mother's house.
I wipe the window which reveals our lounge.
Mother is rocking. Her rhythm drives the city
over the cliff. Her rhythm keeps her warm.
She is knitting me a cardigan white as snow.

Her eyes are the windows of a deserted home.
I tap on the ice, but she can't see. I want
to ask her why she settled here, her dream
of travelling to Tibet, to religious air.
Her chair begins to melt, and I am scratching
at ice packed in annual layers which recede
to the beginning of time. A wall topples,
but I have arrived, and I will go on,
digging my spikes into a vertical facade
until I reach a bedroom window, the master-bed
with no master, the mistress of the house, ill.

Pascale Petit

Forty Eight

Once a month I expect that I am pregnant.
My body takes that liberty –
in the street I am full of misgivings, armfuls,
my breasts manage the joy of being painful.

I expect that the gleaning has taken hold,
the warrior gates have closed
and the town turned heavy inside
with its gold, its tarnish of silver.
I expect the little known
to be drumming and corded,
my belly to be amazed and striated
with new boundaries.

There will no going back,
once a month.
Nowhere will the bereft be local.
They will not be in their usual cafés.
They will be overlooking seaports
and their voices will drop with evening
so as not to wake the children.
No one will be childless
nor the haze hide a bay.

There are slip landings in my belly,
the tug of the mollusc love,

its impersonal kiss unfolded
its wish-kiss lying low
left behind when the sea goes out and stops
for my foot to go oops on the slippery rock.

When the blood lies out on its shoal,
when the blood arrives
on the sloop, on the stoop, like a sailor,
like an acrobat, like electricity,
I will say it is not really that.
No, no. I am not ready.

Jane Duran

Upstairs Light

That particular light begins about half-way
upstairs – a brighter daylight than in kitchen,
hall, or living room, less overshadowed and reduced
by neighbours' walls or lilacs given their heads.
It sparkles. It floods the upper stair-well,
the austere landing, bleaches the bedspreads,
slides along walls, glares from the bathroom tiles.
I, at ground level now, remember it longingly.

Philosophically speaking, of course, it still exists
although, because I do not see it now, it seems
a thing of the past; I used to see, from upstairs windows,
the crystal bases of clouds, the sunset, the lupins
next-door-but-two, the winter stars. It lit
the morning ritual of making beds, of making up.
It spiced afternoon love-making. It illumined
the heads of children asleep.

It was a brighter world upstairs.

Molly Holden

From *This Bed My Centre*

There is a hint of sun today in my small wedge of sky, but it
does not touch my room. The sense of segregation is so palpable,
you feel as if at any moment you will be tightly enclosed in a
cocoon of isolation. Except for the milkman, before dawn, there's

no sound of traffic passing by. Everything is negative. You never hear young people singing, speeding recklessly home from late parties, or even the stereophonic calls of philandering tomcats [...] Only the spasmodic screeching a few doors away, that would send cold shivers down anyone's spine. Yet they tell me nobody here ever has severe pain. It's like living in space. But it has its own grim kind of permanence, for we are all here for the term of our unnatural lives.

Ellen Newton

From *Faces in the Water*

Every morning I woke in dread, waiting for the day nurse to go on her rounds and announce from the list of names in her hand whether or not I was for shock treatment, the new and fashionable means of quieting people and of making them realise that orders are to be obeyed and floors are to be polished without anyone protesting and faces are made to be fixed into smiles and weeping is a crime ...

I tried to remember the incidents of the day before. Had I wept? Had I refused to obey an order from one of the nurses? Or, becoming upset at the sight of a very ill patient, had I panicked, and tried to escape? Had a nurse threatened, 'If you don't take care you'll be for treatment tomorrow?' Day after day I spent the time scanning the faces of the staff as carefully as if they were radar screens which might reveal the approach of the fate that had been prepared for me.

Janet Frame

From *Lost in Translation*

The worst losses come at night. As I lie down in a strange bed in a strange house – my mother is a sort of housekeeper here, to the ageing Jewish man who has taken us in return for her services – I wait for that spontaneous flow of inner language which used to be my night-time talk with myself ... Nothing comes. Polish, in a short time has atrophied, shrivelled from sheer uselessness. Its words don't apply to my new experiences [...]

[...] I have no interior language, and without it, interior images – those images through which we assimilate the external world, through which we take it in, love it, make it our own – become blurred too.

Eva Hoffman

Self-Image and Spiritual Development

From an early age we each build up a picture of who we are, and this is a concept that grows and develops throughout our lives. Sometimes we confound our own expectations, and we must adjust to a changed image. Sometimes it takes a serious knock, and again a modification occurs. Much of the writing an individual does when undertaking any form of self-discovery is likely to have some impact, for good or ill, on the way we see ourselves, and, in the widest sense, on ourselves as spiritual beings.

The first extract, from Virginia Woolf's *Diaries*, finds the author contemplating an aspect of herself which she distrusts, and which adversely affects her maturation as a person and as a writer. It is the traditional feminine role, a learned set of characteristics, to which she is so hostile, and which she claims to have successfully disposed of.

Virginia Woolf identifies two aspects of herself, warring factions in her personality, while Charles Mingus recognizes three. He sees inner self as a battleground between these impulses. The great jazz musician is in conversation with his psychiatrist in this, the opening passage of his autobiography.

The early years are of crucial significance in determining whether aspects of the self-image shall be productive or harmful in later life. In his poem 'Burning Want', Les Murray admits that it took 30 years for him to come to terms with certain social aspects of his schooldays which were to prove chronically inhibiting. In a radio broadcast he admitted that writing it out had proved a therapeutic element in that process.

Joanna Field, in her ground-breaking text, *A Life of One's Own*, tackles the state of her self-knowledge head on. In the extract she describes singing rather than writing, but in her determination to explore her experiences in depth she comes upon a principle which may have application in other areas of her life.

Harold Monro's poem is remarkable for mirroring in its movement the process of a sea-change in the mind. It begins in despair, and ends in confident resolve. There is a strong element of the mysterious in this process.

In considering the various aspects which contribute to one's self-image it becomes obvious that one's passionate enthusiasms play an important part. It may be that one is fortunate enough to have an occupation which harnesses these emotional forces, though for many people they may have to be restricted to their leisure time. Science, sport, art, DIY, cooking – every subject will have its devotees, and one person may espouse a number of them. This aspect of the self-image is represented here in the extract by David Craig. One of his passions is mountain-climbing, and he is lucky enough not only to be a practitioner but also to be sufficiently gifted to be able to write professionally about it as well.

Of course religion may be the overriding impulse in one's life informing everything that one does, in which case no exploration of the self can be complete without full consideration of it.

Even those who have no faith of a formal kind must acknowledge the existence of spiritual experiences and may well value them as highly as anyone with more orthodox beliefs. Our two final examples are taken from the realm of spiritual development but are not denominational in any

sense. The Navajo Indian Chant celebrates irrational experience, a state of ecstasy which has a transforming effect on
the psyche. In its own way so does the poem by Phoebe
Hesketh. She provides a series of images for mental states.
The argument proceeds by feelings rather than thoughts, and
creates the impression of a mystical journeying inwards.

We would also recommend a number of late poems by
Theodore Roethke, one of the most spiritually aware (and
tormented) of contemporary poets. The six sets of medi-
tations under the general title of 'North American Sequence'
express the psychological state of at-oneness wholly in terms
of descriptions so that the landscapes become extended metaphors for the poet's state of mind.

From *Diaries*

She excelled in the difficult arts of family life. If there was chicken
she took the leg; if there was a draught she sat in it. In short she
was so constituted that she never had a mind or a wish of her
own, but preferred to sympathize with the minds and wishes of
others. Above all, I need not say it – she was pure. And when I
came to write, her wings fell on my page: I heard the rustling of
her skirts in the room. She slipped behind me and whispered 'Be
sympathetic; be tender; flatter; deceive; use all the arts and wiles
of your sex. Never let anyone guess you have a mind of your
own. Above all – be pure.' And she made as if to guide my pen.
I now record the one act for which I take some credit to
myself. I turned upon her and caught her by the throat. I did
my best to kill her. My excuse, if I were to be had up in a court
of law, would be that I acted in self-defence. Had I not killed
her, she would have killed me.

Virginia Woolf

From *Beneath the Underdog*

'I am three. One man stands forever in the middle, unconcerned,
unmoved, watching, waiting to be allowed to express what he
sees to the other two. The second man is like a frightened
animal that attacks for fear of being attacked. Then there's an
overloving, gentle person who lets people into the uttermost

sacred temple of his being and he'll take insults and be trusting
and sign contracts without reading them and get talked down
to working cheap or for nothing, and when he realizes what's
been done to him he feels like killing and destroying everything
around him including himself for being so stupid. But he can't
– he goes back inside himself.'
  'Which one is real?'
  'They're ALL real.'

                                                              Charles Mingus

Burning Want

From just on puberty, I lived in funeral:
mother dead of miscarriage, father trying to be dead,
we'd boil sweat-brown cloth; cows repossessed the garden.
Lovemaking brought death, was the unuttered principle.

I met a tall adopted girl some kids thought aloof,
but she was intelligent. Her poise of white-blonde hair
proved her no kin to the squat tanned couple who loved her.
Only now do I realize she was my first love.

But all my names were fat-names, at my new town school.
Between classes, kids did erocide: destruction of sexual morale.
Mass refusal of unasked love; that works. Boys cheered as seventeen-
year-old girls came on to me, then ran back whinnying ridicule.

The slender girl came up on holidays from the city
to my cousins' farm. She was friendly and sane.
Whispers giggled round us. A letter was written as from me
and she was there, in mid-term, instantly.

But I called people 'the humans' not knowing it was rage.
I learned things sidelong, taking my rifle for walks,
recited every scene of *From Here to Eternity*, burned paddocks
and soldiered back each Monday to that dawning Teen age.

She I admired, and almost relaxed from placating,
was gnawed by knowing what she came from, not who.
Showing off was my one social skill, oddly never with her
but I dissembled feelings, till mine were unknown to me too
and I couldn't add my want to her shortfall of wantedness.

I had forty more years, with one dear remission,
of a white paralysis: she's attracted it's not real nothing is enough
she's mistaken she'll die go now! she'll tell any minute she'll
laugh –

Whether other hands reached out to Marion, or didn't,
at nineteen in her training ward she had a fatal accident
alone, at night, they said, with a lethal injection
and was spared from seeing what my school did to the world.

Les Murray

From *A Life of One's Own*

As a child I had been teased for singing out of tune and so all
my life I had felt stupid and thwarted, ashamed to burst into
song whenever I felt like it and deeply envious of those who
could. I could always hear when other people were out of tune
but seemed incapable of producing true notes myself. Then one
day I happened to start humming without thinking about it, for
there was no-one else close enough to overhear, and I suddenly
listened to my own voice and heard that it was in tune. I was
so interested that I went on listening and as long as I listened, so
long did I stay in tune. But as soon as my attention slipped back
to the problem of trying to sing, then my voice wandered off
the note. It seemed that I had always tried to keep in tune by
attending to the muscles in my throat which felt as if they
controlled the sound. After this I found that I could keep in tune
whenever I chose, so long as I thought only of the melody and
forgot that my throat existed.

Joanna Field

Living

Slow bleak awakening from the morning dream
Brings me in contact with the sudden day.
I am alive – this I.
I let my fingers move along my body.
Realization warns them, and my nerves
Prepare their rapid messages and signals.
While Memory begins recording, coding,

Repeating; all the time Imagination
Mutters; You'll only die.

Here's a new day. O Pendulum move slowly!
My usual clothes are waiting on the peg.
I am alive – this I.
And in a moment Habit, like a crane,
Will bow its neck and dip its pulleyed cable,
Gathering me, my body and our garment,
And swing me forth, oblivious of my question,
Into the daylight – why?

I think of all the others who awaken,
And wonder if they go to meet the morning
More valiantly than I;
Nor asking of this Day they will be living:
What have I done that I should be alive?
O can I not forget that I am living?
How shall I reconcile the two conditions:
Living, and yet – to die?

Between the curtains the autumnal sunlight
With lean and yellow fingers points me out;
The clock moans: Why? Why? Why?
But suddenly, as if without a reason,
Heart, Brain and Body, and Imagination
All gather in tumultuous joy together,
Running like children down the path of morning
To fields where they can play without a quarrel:
A country I'd forgotten, but remember,
And welcome with a cry.

O cool glad pasture; living tree, tall corn,
Great cliff, or languid sloping sand, cold sea,
Waves; rivers curving: you, eternal flowers,
Give me content, while I can think of you:
Give me your living breath!
Back to your rampart, Death.

Harold Monro

From *Native Stones*

Even if you walk out into the wilderness there is still a layer of artefact between yourself and nature – the sole of your boot. But to climb is to be intimate with the very stuff of our habitat, to smell its minerals (the struck-match odour of split rock or rock in a heatwave), to imitate the lie of it in the twisting and flexing of your muscles, to relish its most durable elements through the nerves of your fingerends . . . When I sit on a six-inch ledge with my feet dangling above a two-hundred-foot drop, the hart's-tongue fern and dwarf hawthorn a few inches from my eyes, the air smelling of moss, wood-pigeons clattering out of the tree-tops down below, then at least for a time I have grafted myself back into nature, and the sense of rightness achieved, or regained, is unmistakable.

David Craig

The Healing

All the things that have harmed me, they will leave me.
I walk with a cool body after they leave me.
Inside of me today I will be well, all fever will have come out of me, and go away from me, and leave my head cool.
I will hear today, I will see today, I will be in my right mind today.
Today I will walk out.
Today everything evil will leave me, I will be as cool as I was before, I will have a cool breeze over my body, I will walk with a light body.
I will be happy forever, nothing will hinder me.
I will walk with Beauty before me.
I will walk with Beauty above me.
I will walk with Beauty below me.
I will walk with Beauty all around me.
I will walk and speak beautiful words.
I will be forever one, Everything is Beautiful.

Navajo Indian Chant

Credo

I believe in Nothing.

And what is Nothing?
The space within you
where God is,
space between friend and friend,
star and star.
Silence of snowfall
and loved one's absence.

What am I?

A little boat
grappling with angry waves
to keep afloat.
Driven
helpless from shore to shore,
at home only
in the wrench and roar
of waves I defy
that would wrap me in stillness
under storm, under sky
where no winds blow.

I must walk gently
as on a tightrope
now my cup is full,
must balance on air
like a kestrel,
let no drop spill
between dark and dark
as I sing to skylark and sun
lifting up what I hold
to the light.

Phoebe Hesketh

Conclusion

If you have worked your way through this book, first of all – Congratulations! You will have done a great deal of writing, and on the principle that practice is a great teacher you will have learned many strategies for exploring the self through writing. You will also, we feel sure, know rather more about yourself than when you set out on this exploration, and even those things you knew before may well have assumed a new shape or taken up a new place in the pattern of your life. We hope you are experiencing a sense of achievement.

But before you get carried away on an understandable tide of euphoria we should like to pose the question: where do you go from here? We regard the ideas, exercises and examples contained in this book as just the starting-point of an adventure that is life-long. Now that you have demonstrated to yourself some of the ways in which personal writing can contribute to your well-being we hardly need to remind you that there must be more to discover, and that you will have many future experiences which can be filtered and evaluated by your sensibility in ways you have learned to apply. Now that you have acquired the writing habit (or, in the case of those who wrote before, the habit of personal writing), surely living and writing can move in parallel in future, to the mutual benefit of both?

In this book we have concentrated on exploring ways in which the personal can be written about directly. There are other more oblique approaches, such as turning your experience into fiction or drama (which we have touched on), or using myths, legends and fairy stories to illuminate aspects of your life, but limitations of space precluded us from covering these. You may well feel able to embark upon an extended project now: keeping a journal, writing your autobiography, putting together a book of stories or poems ... The only advice we can give you about this is to say – if you *feel* you are ready for such a challenge then you *are* ready.

You will probably wish to explore direct personal writing further and to that end we have appended a reading list. The first part consists of general titles, and this is followed by details of the novels, autobiographies, collections of poetry, etc which we have referred to or quoted from. This is a long list, and we have starred those we particularly recommend.

We have only listed those general works which we have both found useful. They include some outstanding books. For example, *A Life of One's Own* was not only one of the earliest volumes in the field but remains unmatched as an account of a personal voyage of discovery. Similarly, *The New Diary*, though it has been succeeded by other how-to guides on journalling, still seems to us the most creative and helpful book of its kind. Most of the general texts contain reading lists of their own.

As for the second part of our list, we hope that the references to and quotations from these have whetted your appetite for more from these authors. We urge you to follow up as many as you reasonably can. Contrary to popular surmise, reading other writers is not inhibiting; it has been our experience that the stimulus of exploring new subject-matter and seeing new ways of treating familiar concepts constitutes an essential stimulus for self-discovery.

Further Reading

General Books

Field, Joanna (Marion Milner), *A Life of One's Own*, Virago, London, 1986
Fincher, Suzanne F., *Creating Mandalas*, Shambhala, Boston, 1991
Lee, John, *Writing From the Body*, St Martin's Press, New York, 1994
Rainer, Tristine, *The New Diary*, Tarcher, Los Angeles, 1978

Individual Books

Abbs, Peter, *Personae and other poems*, Skoob, London, 1995
——, *The Polemics of Imagination*, Skoob, London, 1996
Angelou, Maya, *I Know Why the Caged Bird Sings*, Virago, London, 1984 *
Atkinson, Donald, *A Sleep of Drowned Fathers*, Peterloo, Calstock, 1989
Bellerby, Frances, *Selected Poems*, Enitharmon, London, 1986 *
Berryman, John, *Selected Poems*, Faber, London, 1972
Bishop, Elizabeth, *Complete Poems 1927–79*, Chatto, London, 1983
——, *Collected Prose*, Chatto, London, 1994
Brittain, Vera, *Testament of Youth*, Virago, London, 1978 *
Brown, Jacqueline, *Thinking Egg*, Arc, Todmorden, 1993 *
Cartwright, Jim, *Bed*, Methuen, London, 1991

Craig, David, *Native Stones*, Secker and Warburg, London, 1987

Davidson, Jonathan, *The Living Room*, Arc, Todmorden, 1994

Deane, Seamus, *Reading in the Dark*, Cape, London, 1996 *

Dillard, Annie, *An American Childhood*, Harper and Rowe, New York, 1987 *

Doty, Mark, *My Alexandria*, Cape, London, 1995

——, *Atlantis*, Cape, London, 1996

——, *Heaven's Coast*, Cape, London, 1996 *

Dunn, Douglas, *Elegies*, Faber, London, 1985 *

Dunn, Sara, Morrison, Blake, Roberts, Michele, *Mind Readings: Writers' Journeys Through Mental States*, Minerva, London, 1996

Duran, Jane, *Breathe Now, Breathe*, Enitharmon, London, 1995

Fanthorpe, Ursula, *Selected Poems*, Peterloo and Penguin, Calstock and London, 1986

Forrester, Helen, *Twopence to Cross the Mersey*, Fontana, London, 1993 *

Frame, Janet, *To the Is-Land*, Flamingo, HarperCollins, London, 1993 *

——, *An Angel at My Table*, Flamingo, HarperCollins, London, 1993*

——, *The Envoy From Mirror City*, Flamingo HarperCollins, London, 1993*

——, *Faces in the Water*, Women's Press, London, 1980 *

Frank, Anne, *The Diary of Anne Frank*, Macmillan, London, 1995 *

Gillilan, Pamela, *Blue Steel Traveller*, Bloodaxe, Newcastle-upon-Tyne, 1994

Hesketh, Phoebe, *The Leave Train*, Enitharmon, London, 1989

Hoffman, Eva, *Lost in Translation*, Minerva, London, 1989 *

Holden, Molly, *Selected Poems*, Carcanet, Manchester, 1989; out of print *

Hopkins, Gerard Manley, *Poems and Prose*, ed. W. H. Gardner, Penguin, London, 1953

Hubbard, Sue, *Everything Begins With the Skin*, Enitharmon, London, 1994

Ignatieff, Michael, *Scar Tissue*, Chatto and Windus, London, 1993 *

Jones, Brian, *The Children of Separation*, Carcanet, Manchester, 1995

Keenan, Brian, *An Evil Cradling*, Vintage/Arrow, London, 1993 *

Keller, Helen, *The Story of My Life*, Hodder & Stoughton, London, 1958

Khalvati, Mimi, *Mirrorwork*, Carcanet, Manchester, 1995

Kirkup, James, *The Only Child*, Collins, London, 1957; out of print *

Lamming, George, *In the Castle of My Skin*, Longman, London, 1979 *

Lawrence, D H, *Sons and Lovers*, Penguin, London, 1962 *

Lazerre, Jane, *The Mother Knot*, Virago, London, 1987 *

Lee, Laurie, *Cider With Rosie*, Penguin, London, 1962 *

Levine, Philip, *What Work Is*, Alfred A Knopf, New York, 1994 *

Lindbergh, Anne Morrow, *A Gift From the Sea*, Vintage/Random House, London, 1991

Macneice, Louis, *The Strings Are False*, Faber, London, 1965

——, *Collected Poems*, Faber, London, 1966

Mansfield, Katherine, *Letters and Journals*, ed C K Stead, Penguin London, 1977 *

Mingus, Charles, *Beneath the Underdog*, Payback Press, Edinburgh, 1995

Mitchell, Elma, *People Etcetera*, Peterloo, Calstock, 1987

Monro, Harold, *Collected Poems*, Duckworth, London, 1970

Moore, Hubert, *Left-Handers*, Enitharmon, London, 1995

Morgan, Edwin, *Collected Poems*, Carcanet, Manchester, 1990

Muir, Edwin, *An Autobiography*, Canongate, Edinburgh, 1993 *

Murray, Les, *Subhuman Redneck Poems*, Carcanet, Manchester, 1996

Newton, Ellen, *This Bed My Centre*, Virago, London, 1980 *

Nimmo, Dorothy, *Homewards*, Giant Steps, Clapham 1987; out of print

Olds, Sharon, *The Father*, Secker and Warburg, London, 1993

——, *The Wellspring*, Cape, London, 1996 *

Owen, Wilfred, *War Poems and Others*, (includes extracts from letters) Chatto & Windus, London, 1973

Petit, Pascale, first full collection, Enitharmon, London, 1998

Price, Caroline, *Thinking of the Bull Dancers*, Littlewood, Todmorden, 1986

——, *Pictures Against Skin*, Rockingham, Ware, 1994

Rawnsley, Irene, *Shall We Gather at the River?*, Littlewood, Todmorden, 1990*

Roethke, Theodore, *Collected Poems*, Faber, London, 1968

Rowbotham, Colin, *Total Recall*, Littlewood, Todmorden, 1987; out of print

Simpson, Matt, *An Elegy for the Galosherman*, Bloodaxe, Newcastle-upon-Tyne, 1990

Sisson, C H, *Christopher Homm*, Carcanet, Manchester, 1975

Soutar, William, *Diary of a Dying Man*, Chapman, Edinburgh, 1991 *

Thrilling, Isobel, *Spectrum Shift*, Littlewood, Todmorden, 1990 *

Tibble, Anne, *Alone*, Peter Owen, London, 1979 *

Waley, Arthur, *Chinese Poems*, Allen and Unwin, London, 1946

Ward, John, *The Wrong Side of Glory*, Littlewood, Todmorden, 1986

Waterhouse, Keith, *There is a Happy Land*, Sceptre, 1992 *

Welty, Eudora, *One Writer's Beginnings*, Faber, London, 1985

Wicks, Susan, *Driving My Father*, Faber, London, 1995 *

Williams, Alfred, *To Live it is to Know it*, Yorkshire Art Circus, Pontefract, 1987; out of print *

Wilson, Frances, *Close To Home*, Rockingham, Ware, 1993

Woolf, Virginia, *Diaries*, Penguin, London, 1979

* books that are particularly recommended

NOTE

Myra Schneider and John Killick are available to run workshops on Writing For Self-Discovery.

Please contact Myra at:
130 Morton Way, London, England N14 7AL